About
WORLD IN CONFLICT

The international news we hear is often about conflicts, strife, and violence in hotspots around the globe. Many conflicts pit people of one ethnic or religious group against those of another. People fight over power, territory, control, and money. But many conflicts are deeply rooted in the past.

The *World in Conflict* series looks at conflicts around the world, examining each in detail. The series provides readers with the background information necessary to understand how these conflicts started in the first place and how they escalated to become headline news stories. The series takes a broad and deep approach—describing the people involved in each conflict, the history behind each conflict, and efforts to end the conflict.

The conflicts featured in these books may not share many similarities, but all are alike in that they are much more complicated than they appear on the surface. *World in Conflict* tackles these complex stories, providing a fascinating look at what causes people to hate—or get along with—one another.

EAST TIMOR

ISLAND IN TURMOIL

EAST TIMOR

ISLAND IN TURMOIL

by Taro McGuinn

Lerner Publications Company / Minneapolis

Website address: www.lernerbooks.com

All maps by Philip Schwartzberg, Meridian Mapping, Minneapolis.
Cover photo by Reuters/Richard Ellis/Archive Photos.
Table of Contents photos (from top to bottom) by Reuters/Enny Nuraheni/Archive Photos; Reuters/David Gray/Archive Photos; photographer unknown; International Committee of the Red Cross.

Series Consultant: Andrew Bell-Fialkoff
Editorial Director: Mary M. Rodgers
Editor: Martha Kranes
Designer: Michael Tacheny
Photo Researcher: Gina Germ

Our thanks to Elaine Briére, Steve Cox, and Andrew McNaughtan for their help in preparing this book.

LIBRARY OF CONGRESS CATALOGING-IN-PUBLICATION DATA

McGuinn, Taro.
East Timor : island in turmoil / Taro McGuinn.
p. cm. — (World in conflict)
Includes bibliographical references and index.
Summary: Examines the history of ethnic conflict in East Timor and its continuing effect on the people.
ISBN 0-8225-3555-6 (lib. bdg. : alk. paper)
1. Timor Timur (Indonesia)—History—Juvenile literature. 2. Timor Timur (Indonesia)—Ethnic relations—Juvenile literature. [1. Timor Timur (Indonesia)] I. Title. II. Series.
DS646.59.T55M42 1998
959.8'6—dc21 97-13683

Manufactured in the United States of America
1 2 3 4 5 6 - JR - 03 02 01 00 99 98

CONTENTS

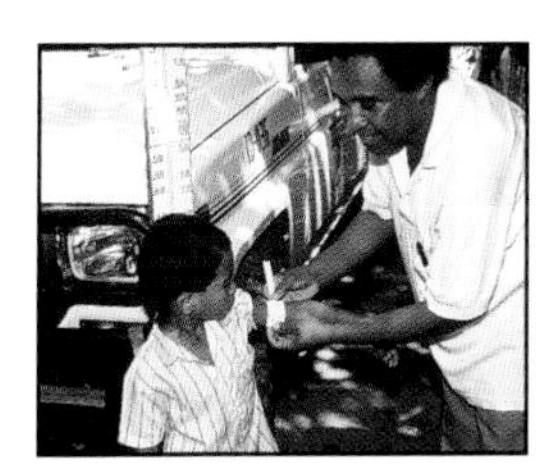

ABOUT THIS SERIES

Government firepower kills 25 protesters .... Thousands of refugees flee the country .... Rebels attack capital .... Racism and rage flare .... Fighting breaks out .... Peace talks stall .... Bombing toll rises to 52 .... Slaughter has cost up to 50,000 lives.

Conflicts between people occur across the globe, and we hear about some of the more spectacular and horrific episodes in the news. But since most fighting doesn't directly affect us, we often choose to ignore it. And even if we do take the time to learn about these conflicts—from newspapers, magazines, television news, or radio—we're often left with just a snapshot of the conflict instead of the whole reel of film.

Most news accounts don't tell you the whole story about a conflict, focusing instead on the attention-grabbing events that make the headlines. In addition, news sources may have a preconceived idea about who is right and who is wrong in a conflict. The stories that result often portray one side as the "bad guys" and the other as the "good guys."

The *World in Conflict* series approaches each conflict with the idea that wars and political disputes aren't simply about bullies and victims. Conflicts are complex problems that can often be traced back hundreds of years. The people fighting one another have complicated reasons for doing so. Fighting erupts between groups divided by ethnicity, religion, and nationalism. These groups fight over power, money, territory, control. Sometimes people who just want to go about their own business get caught up in a conflict just because they're there.

These books examine major conflicts around the world, some of which are very bloody and others that haven't involved a lot of violence. They portray the people involved in and affected by conflicts. They describe how each conflict got started, how it developed, and where it stands. The books also outline some of the ways people have tried to end the conflicts. By reading the stories behind the headlines, you will learn some reasons why people hate and fight one another and, in addition, why some people struggle so hard to end conflicts.

WORDS YOU NEED TO KNOW

anticolonialism: A movement interested in liberating territories from the administration of a colonizing country and restoring self-rule to the inhabitants of that area.

dependency: A relationship between a territory and a country in which the country has control over the territory—provides monetary and military resources—but the territory doesn't officially belong to the country.

enclave: An area or group that is culturally distinct from its surroundings, whether or not the area or group is enclosed within a foreign country.

ethnic group: A permanent group of people bound together by a combination of cultural markers, which may include—but are not limited to—race, nationality, tribe, religion, language, customs, and historical origins.

guerrilla: A rebel fighter, usually not associated with an internationally recognized government, who engages in irregular warfare. Membership in a guerrilla group usually indicates radical, aggressive, or unconventional activities.

nationalism: A feeling of loyalty or patriotism toward one's nation, with a primary emphasis on the promotion of a national culture and national interests.

nationalist movement: An organized effort devoted to achieving independence of a particular group or territory based on its unique cultural traits.

occupation: The holding of a territory by foreign military force against that territory's will.

self-determination: The free choice, without external compulsion, of a people within a territorial unit to decide their own political status.

sovereignty: Power over a region. In some cases, an outside political entity holds the power; in others, a region has its own independent political control.

FOREWORD

by Andrew Bell-Fialkoff

Conflicts between various groups are as old as time. Peoples and tribes around the world have fought one another for thousands of years. In fact our history is in great part a succession of wars—between the Greeks and the Persians, the English and the French, the Russians and the Poles, and many others. Not only do states or ethnic groups fight one another, so do followers of different religions—Catholics and Protestants in Northern Ireland, Christians and Muslims in Bosnia, and Buddhists and Hindus in Sri Lanka. Often ethnicity, language, and religion—some of the main distinguishing elements of culture—reinforce one another in characterizing a particular group. For instance, the vast majority of Greeks are Orthodox Christian and speak Greek; most Italians are Roman Catholic and speak Italian. Elsewhere, one cultural aspect predominates. Serbs and Croats speak dialects of the same language but remain separate from one another because most Croats are Catholics and most Serbs are Orthodox Christians. To those two groups, religion is more important than language in defining culture.

We have witnessed an increasing number of conflicts in modern times—why? Three reasons stand out. One is that large empires—such as Austria-Hungary, Ottoman Turkey, several colonial empires with vast holdings in Asia, Africa, and America, and, most recently, the Soviet Union—have collapsed. A look at world maps from 1900, 1950, and 1998 reveals an ever-increasing number of small and medium-sized states. While empires existed, their rulers suppressed many ethnic and religious conflicts. Empires imposed order, and local resentments were mostly directed at the central authority. Inside the borders of empires, populations were multiethnic and often highly mixed. When the empires fell apart, world leaders found it impossible to establish political frontiers that coincided with ethnic boundaries. Different groups often claimed territories inhabited by others. The nations created on the lands of a toppled empire were saddled with acute border and ethnic problems from their very beginnings.

The second reason for more conflicts in modern times stems from the twin ideals of freedom and equality. In the United States, we usually think of freedom as "individual freedom." If we all have equal rights, we are free. But if you are a member of a minority group and feel that you are being discriminated against, your group's rights and freedoms are also important to you. In fact, if you don't have your "group freedom," you don't have full individual freedom either.

After World War I (1914–1918), the allied western nations, under the guidance of U.S. president Woodrow Wilson, tried to satisfy group rights by promoting minority rights. The spread of frantic nationalism in the 1930s, especially among disaffected ethnic minorities, and the catastrophe of World War II (1939–1945) led to a fundamental reassessment of the Wilsonian philosophy. After 1945 group rights were downplayed on the assumption that guaranteeing individual rights would be sufficient. In later decades, the collapse of multiethnic nations like Czechoslovakia, Yugoslavia, and the Soviet Union—coupled with the spread of nationalism in those regions—came as a shock to world leaders. People want democracy and individual rights, but they want their group rights, too. In practice, this means more conflicts and a cycle of secession, as minority ethnic groups seek their own sovereignty and independence.

The fires of conflict are often further stoked by the media, which lavishes glory and attention on independence movements. To fight for freedom is an honor. For every Palestinian who has killed an Israeli, there are hundreds of Kashmiris, Tamils, and Bosnians eager to shoot at their enemies. Newspapers, television and radio news broadcasts, and other media play a vital part in fomenting that sense of honor. They magnify each crisis, glorify rebellion, and help to feed the fire of conflict.

The third factor behind increasing conflict in the world is the social and geographic mobility that modern society enjoys. We can move anywhere we want and can aspire—or so we believe—to be anything we wish. Every day the television tantalizingly dangles the prizes that life can offer. We all want our share. But increased mobility and ambition also mean increased competition, which leads to antagonism. Antagonism often fastens itself to ethnic, racial, or religious differences. If you are an inner-city African American and your local grocer happens to be Korean American, you may see that individual as different from yourself—an intruder—rather than as a person, a neighbor, or a grocer. This same feeling of "us" versus "them" has been part of many an ethnic conflict around the world.

Many conflicts have been contained—even solved—by wise, responsible leadership. But unfortunately, many politicians use citizens' discontent for their own ends. They incite hatred, manipulate voters, and mobilize people against their neighbors. The worst things happen when neighbor turns against neighbor. In Bosnia, in Rwanda, in Lebanon, and in countless other places, people who had lived and worked together and had even intermarried went on a rampage, killing, raping, and robbing one another with gusto. If the appalling carnage teaches us anything, it is that we should stop seeing one another as hostile competitors and enemies and accept one another as people. Most importantly, we should learn to understand why conflicts happen and how they can be prevented. That is why *World in Conflict* is so important—the books in this series will help you understand the history and inner dynamics of some of the most persistent conflicts of modern times. And understanding is the first step to prevention. 🌐

INTRODUCTION

East Timor—part of the island of Timor—is a small, dry place. Not many people live there or even near there. Yet the fate of this half of an island near the eastern end of Indonesia has been the subject of international controversy since the 1970s.

Timor Island is part of a huge archipelago (island chain) of about 13,600 islands in Southeast Asia between the Indian Ocean and the South Pacific Ocean. Most of the archipelago belongs to the Republic of Indonesia, which stretches east to west for more than 3,200 miles. Timor is in an island group called the Lesser Sundas, which include nearby Flores and Solor. Less than 400 miles southeast of Timor across the Timor Sea sits mainland Australia.

East Timor (population 825,000) includes roughly the eastern half of Timor Island and Ocussi, a small pocket of land on the northern coast of West Timor. East Timor covers 5,635 square miles—slightly larger than the state of Connecticut. West Timor (7,335 square miles) is officially considered part of the Indonesian province of East Nusa Tenggara (the Eastern Southeast Islands). Disagreement about whether East Timor also belongs to Indonesia lies at the heart of the island's conflict.

East Timor has a long history as part of Portugal's colonial empire. For hundreds of years, faraway rulers in Portugal administered the territory. The Portuguese colonial government and military retreated to a nearby island and later withdrew from East Timor in 1975 but never officially declared the territory independent.

For a short period of time after the Portuguese withdrew, a local political group administered the colony. It was called Frente Revolucionaria de Timor-Leste Independente (Fretilin), meaning Revolutionary Front for an Independent East Timor. But in late 1975, Indonesia stepped in and has controlled East Timor militarily ever since.

By the 1700s, Dutch colonizers claimed most of the archipelago, including West Timor, and the Portuguese controlled East Timor. After Indonesia gained independence from the Netherlands in 1949, it laid claim to all former Dutch territories, which included West Timor, but not Portuguese-owned East Timor.

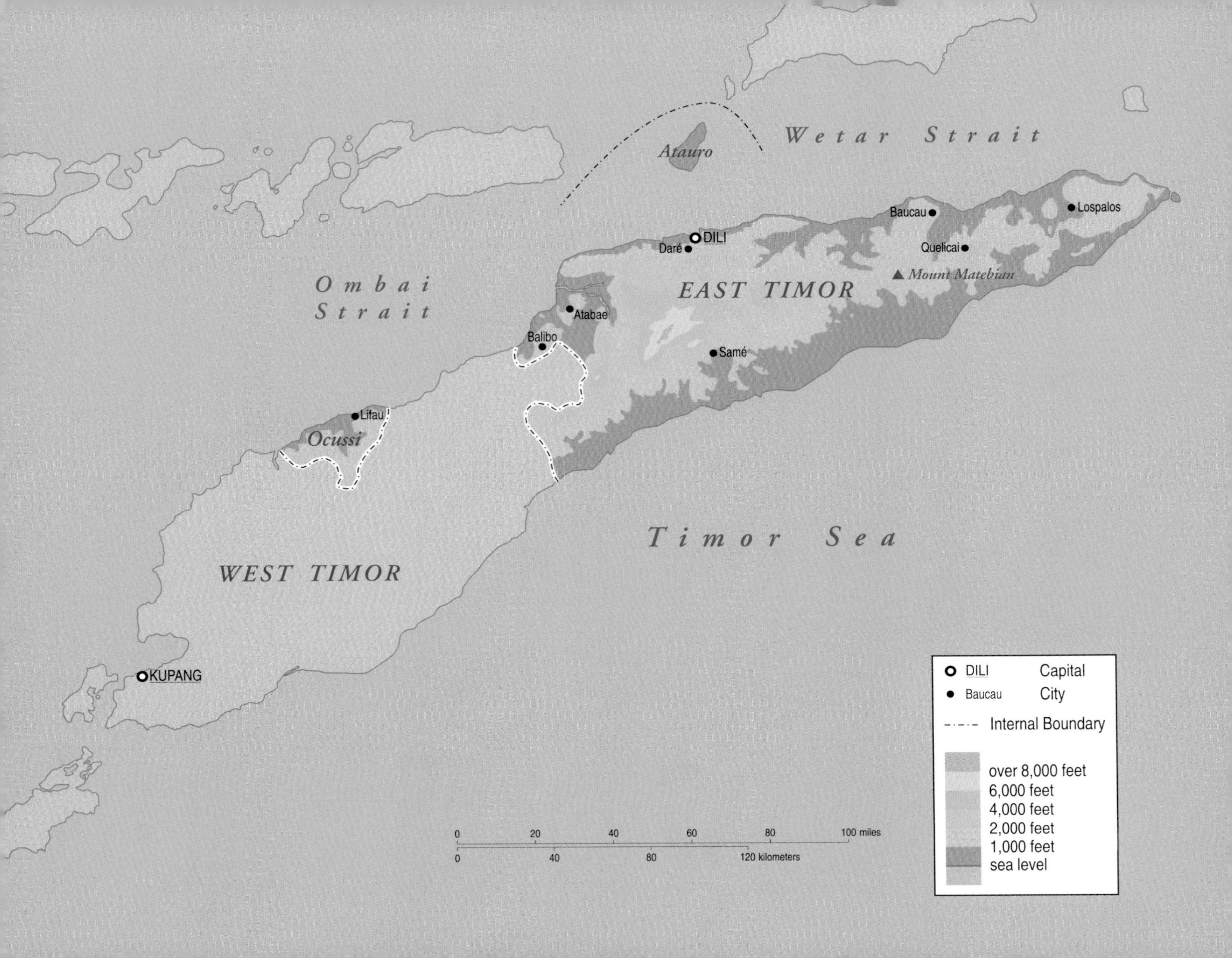

Wetar Strait
Atauro
Ombai Strait
Baucau
Lospalos
DILI
Daré
Quelicai
Mount Matebian
EAST TIMOR
Atabae
Balibo
Samé
Lifau
Ocussi
Timor Sea
WEST TIMOR
KUPANG
DILI Capital
Baucau City
Internal Boundary
over 8,000 feet
6,000 feet
4,000 feet
2,000 feet
1,000 feet
sea level
0 20 40 60 80 100 miles
0 40 80 120 kilometers

The Eastern East

In the Indonesian language, *timor* (sometimes spelled *timur)* means "east." The island got its name because it's the easternmost large island in a long chain stretching from Sumatra in the west to the Lesser Sundas in the east. Consequently, East Timor—the English name for the eastern end of the island—means "eastern east."

This redundancy shows up even in Timor Timur, the official Indonesian term for what that nation considers its twenty-seventh province. In ordinary speech, Indonesians usually shorten the name to "TimTim" or "TT."

Another label applied by the Indonesians to the territory is Loro Sae, meaning "where the sun rises." This name is used only in official documents. Although East Timorese apply Loro Sae to the eastern end of East Timor, adoption by the Indonesians has tarnished this phrase. Instead the East Timorese sometimes call their territory by the outlawed Portuguese name Timor Leste.

Indonesia considers East Timor its twenty-seventh province and calls the territory Timor Timur. It has a capital in Dili on the northern coast. A few nations, including nearby Australia, support Indonesia's claim to the territory. Most members of the United Nations (UN) still view East Timor as a Portuguese possession. The East Timorese want to decide for themselves.

TERRAIN AND CLIMATE

Grassland and low brush cover most of the island's unfarmed areas. Some lush tropical forests grow on the southern slopes of the mountains of Timor, but most of the island's wooded areas have open stands of such dry-climate trees as eucalyptus and acacia.

A mountainous spine runs the length of Timor Island. In parts of East Timor, the peaks edge right up to the sea. The island has few coastal plains. The most notable lies near the border between West and East Timor.

Lying just south of the equator, Timor has warm temperatures year round. The climate is dry, punctuated by seasonal rain. Heavy rains fall during the west monsoon, which blows from November to March. The wettest parts of the island are in the southeast. Some parts of northern and western Timor have a very short wet season, if the rains arrive at all. When rain does fall, it runs off Timor's hard soil—instead of soaking in—and can cause serious erosion.

The short, narrow rivers of East Timor drop steeply to the sea from their mountain sources. The rivers run fast and strong during rainy periods but lessen dramatically in volume and sometimes disappear completely during dry times. None is navigable deep into the interior.

The division between East Timor and West Timor is primarily political. No physical feature distinguishes the two. Long ago a cultural divide separated two powerful **sovereignties** on the island. Later the Portuguese and the Dutch (who colonized West Timor) divided the island roughly at that boundary.

Dili, the largest city in East Timor, has a population of 170,000. Once the Portuguese colonial capital, Dili became the hub of the Indonesian administration for the province of Timor Timur in 1976. Dili also serves as the region's hub for trading sandalwood and coffee, as well as other products from the interior.

ECONOMIC ACTIVITY

East Timor's economy is based on agriculture. Farmers grow subsistence crops, including rice, sweet potatoes, corn, beans, and green vegetables, to feed their families and to sell at local markets. Rice and other staples are routinely imported because regional harvests often fall short of the population's needs. Wheat and potatoes grow well in some of the highland areas. Small orchards produce citrus fruits for the local marketplaces, which also sell locally grown bananas and pineapples. Many farmers raise livestock such as buffalo, goats, and chickens.

Exports of coffee, cotton, copra (the dried insides of

Peter Williamson

Reuters/Enny Nuraheni/Archive Photos

Most of Timor Island is covered with rugged, mountainous terrain (top). *An East Timorese youth* (right) *tends his family's herd of water buffalo.*

coconuts), and beef contribute to East Timor's economy. Coffee, by far the island's most important cash crop, accounts for about 80 percent of the value of all East Timor's exports. Sandalwood was originally Timor's number one export. But by the late 1800s, the sandalwood tree had almost disappeared. Regulated harvesting in the twentieth century has revived the species.

PT Denok

Small plantations operated by local farmers produce the most coffee, but a single large Indonesian company called PT Denok Hernandes (known as PT Denok) controls all areas of the coffee export market, including transportation and the running of large-scale coffee plantations. The owners of PT Denok are officers in the Indonesian military. The company buys coffee from farmers at a low price and then sells it overseas for a large profit. Local farmers who want to sell coffee must do so through PT Denok. The Indonesian military backs the company's policies. In the 1980s, PT Denok diversified into other areas and took over much of the sandalwood trade (as well as trade in cumin, copra, and cloves).

Rich offshore oil and gas reserves lie in the Timor Sea. The Australian and Indonesian governments signed an agreement in 1989 that gave both countries an interest in any oil taken from the Timor Sea. The fields have been parceled out to several international oil companies for exploration and development. Some towns on East Timor's southern coast have expanded as a result of oil exploration, but most of the oil-related growth has occurred in West Timor.

Timor has no substantial deposits of minerals other than petroleum. Small-scale manufacturing produces goods for local use.

Adam Hannestad

Rows of oil drums in Dili await export. Although petroleum is extracted from the seafloor off of East Timor's shores, the territory sees little profit from oil export.

A DIVERSE POPULATION

Several different ethnic groups inhabit East Timor, but modern East Timorese refer to themselves as Maubere. Although the term doesn't refer to an ethnic group, the East Timorese use it to distinguish themselves from Indonesians.

Maubere—a very common man's name—has taken on the meaning of "the common people." It is an affectionate term that suggests someone of humble origins but of trustworthy character.

The indigenous peoples of Timor are classified into two groups—non-Austronesian and Austronesian. The non-Austronesians are found mainly at the eastern end of East Timor and in the central interior. Austronesians share cultural similarities with most of the peoples of Indonesia. One of the largest Austronesian groups in East Timor is the Tetum. Approximately 70,000 Tetum live in East Timor in two areas, one near the border with West Timor and another along the island's southern coast.

The Mambai, another large Austronesian ethnic group in East Timor, inhabit a mountainous area between Dili on the northern coast and Samé on the southern coast. Other smaller indigenous groups include the Tocodote, Ema (or Kemak), Galoli, Makassae, and Idate.

Only a few people in East Timor are of entirely Portuguese ancestry, but many East Timorese have at least one Portuguese ancestor. A number of East Timorese, including many modern political leaders, are half Portuguese and half Timorese. These people of mixed Asian and European heritage are called *mestiços.* Some mestiços have African, Portuguese, and Timorese ancestors.

AP/Wide World Photos

East Timor's population includes several indigenous peoples. This girl is a descendent of the Tetum, also known as the Belu.

Other ethnic groups in East Timor include the Chinese, the Arabs, and the Malays. Although Chinese trade links with Timor date back nearly a thousand years, Chinese traders were not allowed to settle on the island until the time of Portuguese colonial rule. They have since become a big part of the Timorese business community. A small Arab population, living mostly in Dili, claims to be descended from sea traders from the Middle East. Of similar background are some Malays whose ancestors came from the Malay Peninsula before the Indonesian takeover. East Timor's population also includes some Rotinese, Alorese, and other peoples of nearby islands, whose ancestors arrived in East Timor before the Indonesian **occupation.**

About 15 percent of the people living in East Timor are recent arrivals under Indonesia's transmigration program. The program encourages families to move from crowded Indonesian islands to the archipelago's more sparsely populated ones such as East Timor.

LANGUAGES AND RELIGIONS

The traditional languages of East Timor's original inhabitants have survived despite outside influences. Portuguese was widely spoken during colonial rule, but Indonesia banned it in 1981. Bahasa Indonesia, the official language of Indonesia, is taught in schools and is spoken in government. Most young East Timorese can speak it well, but many people who can use Bahasa Indonesia refuse to do so as a form of protest to the Indonesian occupation. The local language of Tetum, once used in trade during Portuguese rule, has become the common language among the East Timorese. Besides being a symbol of Timorese **nationalism,** it is also the language of worship for the Roman Catholic Church in East Timor.

Many transmigrants, who are usually referred to as newcomers, are native speakers of Balinese, Javanese, Buginese, or other languages of the Indonesian islands near Java. Besides these languages, the newcomers also speak Bahasa Indonesia. Many transmigrants are Muslim and so follow the Islamic faith. They share cultural traditions with Muslims in the rest of Indonesia. These characteristics set them apart from the East Timorese, who mainly practice the Roman Catholic form of Christianity.

Citizens of Indonesia choose from the five officially recognized religions. They are Catholicism, Islam, Protestantism (one of the Christian denominations), Hinduism (practiced in India), and Buddhism (practiced in many Asian countries). The most important religion of modern-day East Timor is Catholicism. One reason is that the Indonesian authorities require the Timorese to choose from the five officially recognized religions and Catholicism is the most familiar option. But many East Timorese are genuinely attracted to the Catholic Church as one of the few institutions able to criticize the Indonesian authorities without severe retaliation. Since the Indonesian takeover in 1975, membership in the

Catholic parishioners leave a church (facing page) *after morning mass. Portuguese colonizers introduced Catholicism to the territory, but it wasn't widely practiced until after the Indonesian invasion, when membership more than doubled. Christianity has not completely replaced native religions, in which natural features have spiritual significance.*

Islam is a religion that was established in the seventh century. Its followers are called Muslims, and Islam is based upon the teachings of the Prophet Mohammed. The religion was brought to the Indonesian archipelago in the fifteenth century by Arab traders, but Islam made very few converts among the Timorese. Indonesia as a whole is more than 80 percent Muslim, but in East Timor only about 3 percent of the people practice Islam. Religion creates a significant cultural split between East Timor and Indonesia.

Reuters/Enny Nuraheni/Archive Photos

Catholic Church has risen dramatically in East Timor. By 1994 more than 90 percent of East Timor's people had become Catholic. Membership in the Catholic Church functions as a potent symbol of resistance because the Indonesian government is strongly associated with Islam.

THE NATURE OF THE CONFLICT

In 1975, shortly after the Portuguese retreated to a nearby island, East Timor erupted in civil war. Local factions with differing ideas of how the territory should be run turned against one another. For several months, these factions fought for control of the territory. Fretilin fought against a coalition of groups made up of the União Democratica Timorense (UDT) and Associação Popular Democratica Timorense (Apodeti). The coalition was backed—at first secretly and later outwardly—by the Indonesian armed forces.

After Fretilin declared independence in November 1975, Indonesia saw an opportunity to invade, stating that Fretilin forces had overturned Portuguese rule. The Indonesians also claimed that the East Timorese people had called for their help in restoring peace. Indonesia, accepting a request from the small integrationist coalition (which included the UDT), annexed (took over) East Timor as part of Indonesia in 1976. Indonesian officials helped create a provincial government made up of members of the UDT and Apodeti. They also installed Indonesian troops in East Timor to maintain order.

Reuters/Stringer/Archive Photos

In 1994 police in riot gear lined the streets outside the University of East Timor, in Dili, while students staged a demonstration against the occupation inside the campus walls. Indonesian soldiers have been patrolling the streets since before most of the students were born.

One of the aspects of Indonesian occupation that the East Timorese most object to is the failure to be asked for their opinion. They do not want to stand by again as another large government assumes to know what is best for East Timor. The current conflict centers mainly on East Timor's struggle to establish a separate national identity. And in the process of defining themselves, the East Timorese hope to secure for themselves the right to determine their own future.

The conflict is multifaceted, and ethnic tensions add to the complexity of the situation. The East Timorese feel dissimilar, both ethnically and culturally, from the occupying Indonesians. They come from different **ethnic groups** than the peoples of Indonesia, and they were influenced by Portuguese colonial rule, whereas Indonesia was colonized by the Dutch.

Religion comes into play, although the conflict is not strictly defined by clashes of faith. A large majority of Indonesians are Muslim, and the East Timorese are Catholic. Occasionally, religious views fuel struggles between Indonesian soldiers and East Timorese protesters. But as it stands, East Timor's troubles are a secular (non-religious) conflict between people who happen to be strongly religious. In fact, the struggle in East Timor could be called a **nationalist movement,** which means that the East Timorese are fighting to preserve their own language and culture.

As the number of Indonesian transmigrants to the area has risen, a cultural conflict on the island has intensified. Most jobs and much of the land taken away from the

Shortly after Indonesia took over the territory, hundreds of East Timorese citizens gathered to back the pro-independence party, Fretilin. Indonesia claimed that the independence movement had only a few, outspoken supporters.

Penny Tweedie/Panos Pictures

East Timorese who were placed in prison camps during the takeover go to these newcomers. This practice has built resentment between the East Timorese and the Indonesians. What was once a political and military struggle has taken on ethnic and religious undertones.

POLITICAL GROUPS

The people of East Timor have become the focus of a political controversy few of them want. There are two major camps in East Timor—those who want to integrate with Indonesia, and those who want independence. Some may want uncompromising independence from Indonesia. Others may fear that total autonomy would bring more hardships for East Timor. Most average East Timorese fall somewhere in between. But one thing they all agree on is that they want to end the violence and disrespect for East Timorese culture that has typified the Indonesian occupation.

The integrationists believe that East Timor cannot survive without the help of Indonesia. By integrating, the East Timorese would depend on Indonesia economically, politically, and militarily. Many of those who prefer integration are members of the Indonesian-sponsored government, or who have benefited from the Indonesian occupation. However, while they may like the idea of integration in theory, they disagree with the violence that has accompanied the Indonesian occupation thus far.

Governor Abilio Soares—a member of the UDT—and other East Timorese members of the installed government must answer to the Indonesian central government, which operates from the capital city of Jakarta on the island of Java. Some of these government officials attempt to speak out against the brutality of the armed forces, but the Indonesian military keeps the Timorese leaders from saying or doing much. Indonesian forces in East Timor account for between 7,000 soldiers (the Indonesian government's estimate) and 30,000 (the claim of independence groups). The popularity of the Indonesian-approved government has never been tested in a fair election.

On the other hand, a large number of East Timorese would like independence from Indonesia. Various groups are working to promote this aim. The most well-organized is a coalition of independence groups called the National Council of Maubere Resistance (CNRM, based on its East Timorese name). The council operates from huts in the mountains with help from East Timorese exiles living in other countries. Established in 1986, this coalition consists of some small independence groups and Fretilin.

Fretilin formed in 1974 and has been a long-standing force in the nationalist movement. From the beginning, Fretilin has been the independence group most willing to use violence to achieve freedom. Outnumbered by the Indonesian army, Fretilin fighters have used their knowledge of East Timor's rugged terrain to their advantage. By employing guerrilla warfare tactics—such as surprise attacks and ambushes—Fretilin has managed to maintain positions in the interior. The number of actual **guerrillas** in the

East Timor's resistance fighters are willing to use violence to fight Indonesian occupation. Over the years, the guerrillas' ability to remain hidden has been to their advantage—especially when staging surprise attacks on Indonesian soldiers.

Fretilin movement is impossible to know. The Indonesian estimate, about 200, is probably too low, while the Fretilin estimate of 3,000 is probably too high. Fretilin does enjoy international recognition, largely because of the public relations work of one of its members, José Ramos-Horta, a political refugee who speaks for East Timor from his office in Australia.

In 1997 Fretilin leader Konis Santana took a surprising stand for the pro-independence group. In the interest of finding a solution, he proposed that East Timor could have an association with Indonesia—a relationship similar to the one between Puerto Rico and the United States. Puerto Rico, a commonwealth, maintains loose political ties with the United States but has full control of its own government policies. Indonesia refused to accept the proposal, stating that Fretilin represents a minority of East Timorese.

While the active membership of the CNRM is relatively small, the East Timor Catholic Church functions locally as a mouthpiece for the resistance movement.

José Ramos-Horta

Reuters/Pierre Virot/Archive Photos

José Ramos-Horta was born just after Christmas in 1949 in Dili. He went into exile in Australia after the Indonesian invasion in 1975, and he has remained outside the territory ever since. He would almost certainly be arrested if he returned to East Timor.

Although his advocacy of East Timorese liberty won him a share of the 1996 Nobel Peace Prize, José Ramos-Horta hasn't spent any time in East Timor since the 1970s. His residences and offices are in Australia and Portugal, and he spends much of his time traveling internationally in his anti-Indonesian crusade.

This lifestyle leaves him open to a lot of criticism from the Indonesian authorities. Whereas his corecipient of the 1996 peace prize, Bishop Belo, was respectfully (if cautiously) congratulated by Indonesian authorities, Ramos-Horta was denounced as a high-living opportunist. Indonesian campaigns against Ramos-Horta have featured charges that he misuses funds donated to the Timorese cause and exploits the issue to maintain a glamorous international lifestyle. Ramos-Horta denies these charges.

Since his early twenties, the linguistically gifted Ramos-Horta has been a public figure who is comfortable making presentations to crowds and panels of officials. (His native language is Tetum, but he also speaks Portuguese, English, French, and Spanish.) One of the founders of Fretilin, he was soon entrusted with public relations functions such as newsletters, speech writing, and international expeditions to drum up support for the cause. His current position as spokesperson for the National Council of Maubere Resistance (CNRM) is the natural outgrowth of this career.

Peter Williamson

Bishop Carlos Felipe Ximenes Belo

A joint recipient of the Nobel Peace Prize in 1996, Bishop Belo was born in the East Timorese city of Baucau in 1946. After studying at Our Lady of Fatima Seminary at Daré, south of Dili, he went to Portugal and Italy to train for the Roman Catholic priesthood. He joined a group of Catholics called the Salesian Order, who specialize in helping disadvantaged youth, and studied at a Salesian university in Rome. He was ordained in Lisbon, the capital of Portugal, in 1980.

Belo returned to East Timor in 1981 and began working in his hometown of Baucau at a secondary school called Fatumaca College. In 1983, while Belo was serving as director of this school, Pope John Paul II presented him with a great challenge—to take over as the apostolic administrator (the Pope's personal representative) in East Timor. Belo officially became a bishop in 1988 when the Pope appointed him Bishop of Lorium—a suburb of Rome.

Before coming to East Timor, Belo was a low-profile, apolitical figure. He has surprised many people with his activism and his willingness to speak for the East Timorese. Yet he has disappointed some of East Timor's more radical dissidents by working within limits set by the territory's Indonesian administration. Belo's practical, balanced approach has nonetheless been very successful in attracting international sympathy to the East Timorese cause. Even before he won the 1996 Nobel Peace Prize, Belo had been proposed for the prize in 1994 and in 1995.

The church cannot officially reject Indonesian rule, but Bishop Carlos Felipe Ximenes Belo—the apostolic administrator in Dili—often criticizes the harsh repression of the East Timorese by Indonesian soldiers and police.

Students and young people have developed a loosely organized popular resistance movement in Dili and in other towns. These protesters often shout support for Fretilin and its jailed former leader, Xanana Gusmão, but their actual connections to Fretilin are tenuous. These young activists represent a new generation of disaffected East Timorese. They have been educated by the Indonesians in the Indonesian language, but because the best jobs go to Indonesians, they feel like outcasts in their own land. As they watch the Indonesian security forces kill or torture more and more of their friends and schoolmates, these young East Timorese grow angrier and more vocal.

Although most East Timorese would probably like Indonesian forces to leave the territory, the exit of the Indonesian military and total independence are not the same thing. The UN still considers the territory to be a **dependency** of Portugal. Would Portuguese rather than Indonesian dependence be preferable for East Timor? Could the East Timorese economy succeed on its own without Indonesian aid? Might the East Timorese choose some sort of loose association with Portugal? Might the East Timorese even choose some relationship with Indonesia, as long as the relationship was theirs by choice?

No one knows. The East Timorese have never had a chance to freely express their wishes. In the final analysis, the conflict in East Timor is primarily a struggle for **self-determination** (the right to decide the status of one's country). The disagreement places local residents, who would like to decide their future for themselves, against an outside authority, the Indonesian government, which claims to know what is best for East Timor.

Reuters/Enny Nuraheni/Archive Photos

Young East Timorese protesters wear clothing and hold a banner displaying the Fretilin flag. Fretilin has operated under the National Council of Maubere Resistance (CNRM) since 1986, but the group's strong anti-Indonesian stance helps it endure as a powerful symbol of protest.

MAJOR PLAYERS IN THE CONFLICT

Peter Williamson

Bishop Belo

Fretilin

Portugal

Belo, Felipe Carlos Ximenes A bishop and apostolic administrator for the Roman Catholic Church in East Timor since 1983. He received the Nobel Peace Prize in 1996, along with José Ramos-Horta, for his work to end Indonesian brutality toward the East Timorese.

Falintil See Fretilin.

Frente Revolucionaria de Timor-Leste Independente (Fretilin) Founded as the Associação Social Democratica Timorense (ASDT) in 1974 but changed its name to Fretilin in 1975. Fretilin declared independence for East Timor shortly before the start of the 1975 civil war. Through the early 1980s, Fretilin and Falintil (its military arm) maintained a strong network of organized resistance. The party remains a potent symbol of East Timorese resistance but has functioned under the National Council of Maubere Resistance since 1982.

National Council of Maubere Resistance (CNRM) Established in 1982 as the Revolutionary Council of National Resistance and renamed CNRM in 1986. The organization unites various anti-Indonesian groups to end the Indonesian occupation of East Timor.

Portugal The colonial ruler of East Timor since the 1700s, Portugal is still considered the official government of East Timor. Portugal never relinquished its territory of East Timor to Indonesia, nor did it grant the territory independence. The country is working with the UN and independently to find a viable solution to the conflict.

Republic of Indonesia Military occupier of East Timor. After troops helped end the civil war in 1975, Indonesian officials installed a government in East Timor, which answers to the central government in Jakarta. Troops of the Indonesian Army have remained on the island since 1975.

Republic of Indonesia

Ramos-Horta, José An East Timor exile since 1975, Ramos-Horta advocates East Timorese independence from his offices in Australia. He is a co-recipient of the 1996 Nobel Peace Prize, is a founding member of Fretilin, and is a spokesperson for the CNRM.

Reuters/Pierre Virot/Archive Photos

José Ramos-Horta

Suharto Served as a general in Indonesia's army under its first president, Sukarno, in the 1960s. Suharto took over the presidency of the Republic of Indonesia in 1968 and was reelected for the sixth consecutive term in 1993. President Suharto granted a request to the provisional government of East Timor in 1976 to become a part of Indonesia.

União Democratica Timorense (UDT) Founded in 1974, the UDT advocated a gradual transition to local rule. During the civil war, the UDT grew dependent on Indonesia and became part of the Indonesian-installed government. Although the UDT has seats in the local government, some of its exiled members work from abroad protesting the Indonesian occupation.

Reuters/Enny Nuraheni/Archive Photos

Suharto

CHAPTER 1

THE RECENT CONFLICT AND ITS EFFECTS

In October 1996, two unfamiliar names rocketed into worldwide headlines. Bishop Carlos Felipe Ximenes Belo and José Ramos-Horta had received one the world's highest honors—the Nobel Peace Prize.

Bishop Belo is a Roman Catholic bishop and a critic of Indonesia's occupation in East Timor. Ramos-Horta is a Fretilin member in exile and an international advocate of independence for East Timor. Both are figures in a conflict that is rarely on the front page, in part because the conflict occurs in an area of the world remote from the biggest cities and media centers. In addition, Indonesia restricted foreign access to the entire territory of East Timor from 1976 through 1988, so very few reports describing conditions there reached the outside world.

When Bishop Belo, far left, *and José Ramos-Horta,* far right, *won the Nobel Peace Prize in 1996, the international media renewed its coverage of the struggle for peace in East Timor.*

LOOKING FOR A VOICE

East Timor's nationalist groups face the military of Indonesia, one of the world's largest and most populous nations. In many cases, soldiers have treated the East Timorese very harshly—seizing property, arresting and imprisoning nonviolent protesters, torturing opponents of Indonesian occupation, and even murdering civilians. The actions of the military anger East Timorese citizens, including those previously uninterested in the nationalist movement. And the Indonesian authorities admit that soldiers have sometimes greatly exceeded the limits of reasonable force.

Demonstrators have often faced harsh treatment from Indonesian authorities. In 1990 police beat student protesters in Dili who had attempted to speak with U.S. ambassador John Monjo about the Indonesian soldiers' treatment of the East Timorese.

The award of the Nobel Peace Prize to East Timorese activists was an unexpected bonus for opponents of the Indonesian occupation—a chance for them to get media attention without risking violence. World attention is vital to the success of East Timorese nationalist groups because their numbers are small, their resources few, and their ability to influence world perception almost nonexistent. This attention usually comes when people are beaten, tortured, or killed. And such events have occurred in East Timor.

For example, the Timorese got attention after John Monjo, the U.S. ambassador to Indonesia, paid a brief visit to Dili in January 1990. During his stay, a group of young East Timorese demonstrators who wanted to speak to Monjo dodged the rifle butts of Indonesian soldiers to approach him in the driveway of the Hotel Turismo. The demonstrators risked violence in order to tell Monjo that Indonesian soldiers were raping, torturing, and murdering East Timorese citizens. After Monjo left, Indonesian troops in riot gear vigorously beat scores of unarmed teenagers huddled against the fence in front of the hotel. Some witnesses report that two students were killed, although the Indonesian government denies this claim.

In another incident on November 12, 1991, East Timorese mourners attended a memorial service in Dili for a civilian, who was killed two weeks earlier by the Indonesian security forces. The mourners were joined by thousands of protesters in a march to the city's Santa Cruz Cemetery. Many people carried anti-Indonesian and pro-Fretilin banners. As mourners and protesters gathered in the cemetery, Indonesian soldiers armed with M16 assault rifles fired randomly into the crowd. The official Indonesian tally of the dead was 50, but other estimates run from 115 to 271 dead.

In 1995—the twentieth anniversary of Indonesia's takeover—demonstrations, rioting, and guerrilla activity continued in East Timor. Of 18 people killed in three months, only two were guerrilla fighters. The rest were civilians. While these numbers may not sound large, they show that regular East Timorese citizens still receive the brunt of Indonesian action against the population.

A report published by Human Rights Watch/Asia in September 1997 told of East Timorese youths recruited to help the Indonesian security forces. The military targets unemployed young people to be informers of anti-integration and guerrilla activity, and to receive military training. A program called Gardapaksi (short for Youth Guard for Upholding Integration) was created in 1995 to provide technical training to out-of-work East Timorese youth. In addition to learning a trade, sources informed, members receive some military training as well. Reportedly, prisoners arrested for anti-integration involvement are released on the condition that they join Gardapaksi. Members are said to be offered monetary and material incentives to take part in counterdemonstrations to pro-independence rallies.

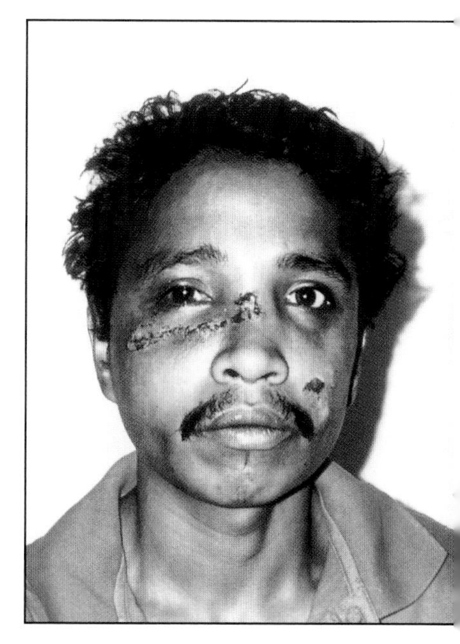

Moments after Indonesian troops fired on demonstrators and mourners (facing page), *in what was called the Dili Massacre, survivors tended to wounded victims in a shelter within the Santa Cruz Cemetery walls. Suspected organizers of the 1991 mass protest were subsequently arrested for questioning. Although cases of torture as an interrogation technique are often hard to verify, photos like this one* (above) *offer proof of the harsh treatment of prisoners.*

The 1997 parliamentary elections in Indonesia (in which Golkar, President Suharto's ruling party, overwhelmingly won) sparked a string of attacks both by and against the East Timorese. Anti-integrationist groups objected to the elections because holding the vote in East Timor presumed the territory's integration with Indonesia. Guerrilla fighters targeted polling places, election officials, and occasionally voters to show their rejection of Indonesian rule. Indonesian forces responded to the attacks by arresting, imprisoning, and torturing prisoners. In the wake of the election violence, the guerrilla force's second-in-command was shot and killed by Indonesian soldiers.

Tensions have continued to escalate, largely in response to the social changes brought about by the Indonesian occupation and by the number of Indonesian immigrants moving to East Timor since the 1980s. Ethnically and religiously motivated clashes between the East Timorese and the Indonesian military, and between the East Timorese and Indonesian transmigrants exemplify the latest breed of violence in the territory. In addition, the 1990s has seen a rise in the amount of violence between anti-integration youth protesters and organized groups of young East Timorese allegedly linked to the Indonesian army.

President Suharto

One of the world's longest-serving heads of state, President Suharto of Indonesia has been in power since 1966. He and his family have a lock, not only on political power in Indonesia but also on much of the business sector.

Suharto (the president's full name) was born in central Java in 1921. He fought beside the Japanese against the Allies during World War II in the hope of driving out the Dutch colonizers. After the war, he was active in the Indonesian independence movement. He built a career in the army, eventually going to an elite school for officers. Because his nationalist politics suited Sukarno, Indonesia's first president, Suharto was given some important assignments. One of these was heading the military units that eventually expelled the Dutch from West Irian, New Guinea, in the early 1960s.

When the Indonesian Communist Party allegedly attempted to overthrow Sukarno's government in 1965, General Suharto leapt to the rescue. His units received credit for putting down the Communist revolt. On the surface, it looked as if Suharto had restored Sukarno to power, but in reality, Sukarno stayed in office as a mere figurehead while Suharto ran the government. What had started out as a Communist revolt turned into a military coup.

Since ousting Sukarno, Suharto has held power with an iron fist, partly by maintaining the army's loyalty. For example, some seats in the national legislature are reserved for the military, and military officers are appointed to political offices at every level. Suharto makes all important appointments himself, so virtually every influential Indonesian feels indebted to the president.

In 1998 Suharto is expected to try for his seventh five-year term as president. If he runs, he is sure to win. But he is nearly 80 years old and is not likely to remain in power much longer. There is no clear sign of who might succeed him. Of his six children, the only one who has pursued a political career is Siti Hardiyanti Rukmana—his eldest daughter and the chair of the central committee of Golkar, Suharto's political organization. But she has not yet shown any presidential ambitions.

Independent Picture Service

Suharto, circa 1970

The 1991 Dili Massacre and the award of the 1996 Nobel Peace Prize drew international attention to East Timor. As a result, the visible violence subsided considerably. But protesters and students suspected of organizing anti-Indonesian rallies still are routinely jailed and questioned, often under torture. As international awareness of East Timor rose, Indonesia occasionally addressed the political situation, but little progress has been made to resolve the conflict.

Although no internationally recognized agreement grants Indonesia political power in East Timor, the country continues to exert authority.

LEGAL ISSUES

Although no internationally recognized agreement grants Indonesia political power in East Timor, the country continues to exert authority. In 1975, after Portugal withdrew from East Timor, Indonesia took military control and set up a temporary government. In 1976 Jakarta accepted a request from the East Timorese to be integrated into Indonesia. The request came from East Timorese factions installed by the Indonesians in the temporary government and not from a freely elected assembly speaking for the general populace. The UN refused to send representatives to Indonesia for the official handover ceremony.

UN/DPI Photo

The UN Security Council, the part of the UN that recommends solutions to international disputes, has advocated several measures to achieve peace in East Timor. Indonesia has ignored all suggestions.

Indonesia still governs East Timor. Indonesians along with Timorese who are part of the Indonesian-approved government run the power stations, control the airports, build and manage the public schools, and perform all the other functions of government. Indonesian military troops patrol the streets, the official currency is the Indonesian ruppiah, and the

Reuters/David Gray/Archive Photos

On the twentieth anniversary of the invasion, a group of East Timorese protesters displayed banners outside of the Indonesian embassy in Sydney, Australia. Although the UN doesn't recognize Indonesia's annexation of East Timor, the Australian government supports Indonesia.

official language is Bahasa Indonesia. But a majority of East Timorese people oppose the Indonesian government, a fact that is evident in the mass outpouring of protesters anytime there is a demonstration.

Since 1976 the UN has voted several times on resolutions to help solve the East Timor conflict. Sometimes the organization has called upon Indonesia to remove its soldiers and at other times it has supported the right of the people of East Timor to self-determination. In all UN resolutions, Indonesia's claim to a legitimate presence in East Timor has been voted down. The official UN position is that East Timor is a non–self-governing possession of Portugal until something else can be decided.

NECESSARY INTERVENTION

Indonesia views its control of East Timor as a practical response to circumstances. The Indonesian government argues that it was forced to act to prevent disaster after Portugal retreated in 1975, leaving a variety of factions to fight for control. One of the more radical factions, Fretilin, was known for its leftist views that sounded like Communist doctrine. Indonesia feared the civil unrest on its borders and was worried about having a Communist state as its neighbor.

Indonesia feared the civil unrest on its borders and was worried about having a Communist state as its neighbor.

Since the collapse of the Soviet Union in 1991, the threat of Communist neighbors has become remote. But in the mid-1970s, Communist take-overs in Vietnam, Laos, and Cambodia had just occurred, and Indonesian officials became seriously concerned about the regional impact. Indonesia feared that if East Timor became a Communist client state, the powerful navy of the Soviet Union would seek a sea route linking Southeast Asian Communist countries to Timor Island. Such a Soviet seaway would cut Indonesia in two, placing a strategic obstacle between the central government in Jakarta and its eastern islands.

A more important consideration—the desire to avoid caving in to pressure from various Indonesian separatist groups that wanted to break away—later motivated Indonesian politicians to hold on to East Timor. Indonesia felt it couldn't grant East Timor autonomy (self-governance) without sending the wrong message to Indonesian separatist groups in Ambon, Irian Jaya, South Sulawesi, and North Sumatra.

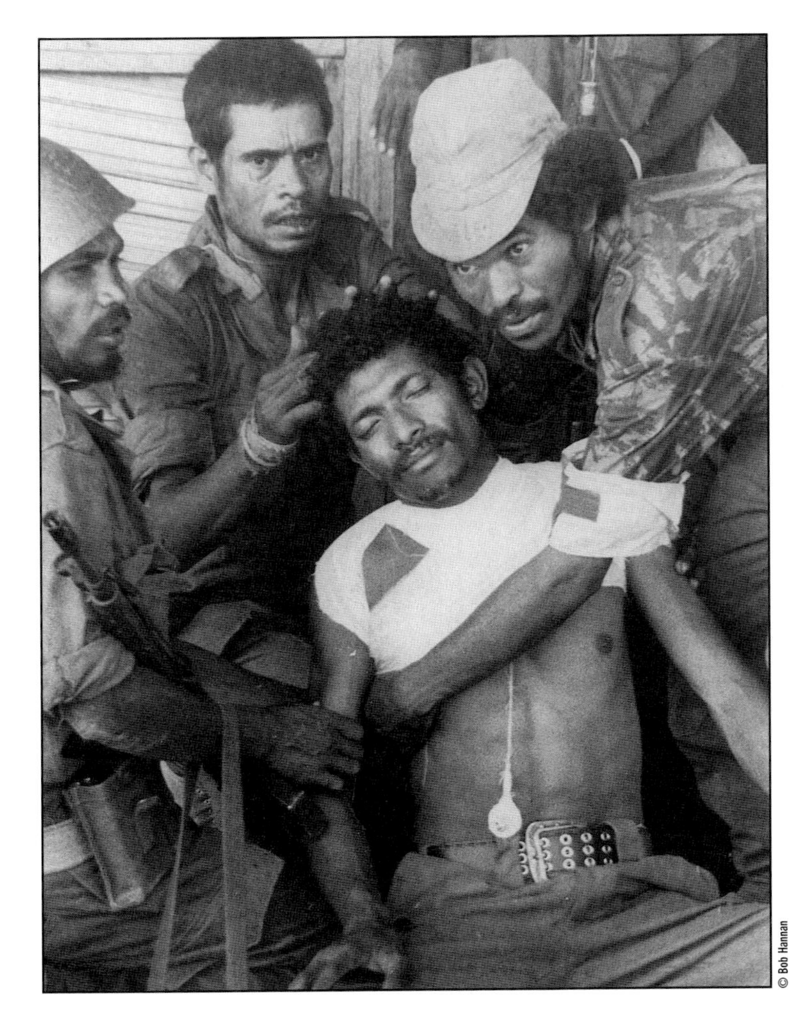

© Bob Hannan

Fretilin soldiers care for a wounded victim of the four-month-long civil war that troubled East Timor after the Portuguese pulled out of the territory in 1975.

From the Indonesian point of view, integration of East Timor makes the most economic sense. By itself the territory is too small, too dry, and too poor to sustain a viable economy. Indonesia also sees a geographic inevitability to the integration of East Timor. Because the rest of the archipelago is under Indonesian jurisdiction, Indonesia doesn't see any political value in allowing this small pocket of non-Indonesian territory to exist within the vast archipelago.

© Steve Cox

Indonesia brought material benefits to East Timor. Despite these benefits, the East Timorese staged a mass protest after 16 years of Indonesian rule.

Indonesia often justifies its annexation of East Timor by pointing to the territory's improved standard of living since the takeover. Under Portuguese rule, the faraway colony was neglected. But after Indonesia took control of the territory, conditions and infrastructure improved. For example, East Timor has more paved roads (1,305 miles in 1994, only 12 miles in 1976) and more schools (815 in 1994, only 51 in 1976). According to Indonesia's president Suharto, the average East Timorese citizen earned 600,000 ruppiah (about U.S. $258) in 1994, as opposed to only 80,000 ruppiah (about U.S. $34) in 1976. East Timor has seen a rise in the number of students getting a university education, a higher life expectancy, and various other indicators of improvement during more than 20 years of Indonesian control.

From the Indonesian point of view, integration makes the most economic sense. East Timor is too small, too dry, and too poor to sustain a viable economy.

A SEPARATE IDENTITY

Indonesia's position assumes that the East Timorese are willing to embrace Indonesian control to enjoy the material comforts Indonesia can bring. But significant numbers of East Timorese participate in anti-Indonesian rallies, indicating that a large segment of the population opposes Indonesia's occupation.

The East Timorese view the situation in more than economic terms. They resent Indonesian control because they consider themselves non-Indonesian in language, religion, history, and law. They fail to see the inevitability of Indonesian rule, and they reject the notion that an independent East Timor could not survive. They point to Singapore and to other former colonies that are much smaller than East Timor, yet have managed to succeed after independence.

When Indonesia became independent of the Netherlands in 1949, its national borders included the archipelago's former Dutch territories, called the Netherlands East Indies. East Timor, however, was a Portuguese colony. Up until 1975, Indonesia repeatedly stated that it was the successor state only to the former Dutch possessions. In 1975 Indonesia occupied East Timor, a territory it had never previously claimed. In the next two decades, 200,000 East Timorese—one third of the population—starved when Indonesian forces destroyed their crops, died of preventable diseases in Indonesian prison camps, or were murdered under Indonesian rule.

Since the award of the Nobel prize in 1996, widespread violence in East Timor has decreased. Indonesian troops have had to watch their actions to avoid attracting negative attention from the international media and from human-rights groups. Out of fear, most East Timorese keep clear of Indonesian soldiers stationed in East Timor. But a growing movement of students and young people continues to call attention to the fact that problems still exist in East Timor despite the award of the Nobel Peace Prize. 

Sparse Vegetation

The sparseness of East Timor's vegetation is due partly to the climate and the rocky soil. Another important factor, however, is the tradition of slash-and-burn agriculture. Farmers cut down the vegetation, burn it, and mix the charred material into the soil as fertilizer.

In addition, eucalyptus forests that once covered Timor's lower hills have been cleared to create cattle ranches. The Indonesian military reportedly killed a lot of East Timor's vegetation in the late 1970s. To make rebels easier to spot, the soldiers sprayed the landscape with chemicals that made the leaves drop off the trees.

The East Timorese view the situation in more than economic terms. They resent Indonesian control because the East Timorese consider themselves non-Indonesian in language, religion, history, and law.

A ritual house of one of Timor's indigenous peoples stands in the hills as a reminder of the traditional ways of life on the island.

Elaine Briére

CHAPTER 2

THE CONFLICT'S ROOTS

Shards of pottery offer evidence that humans lived on Timor Island as far back as 1000 B.C., if not longer. The pottery belonged to peoples whom anthropologists have named Austronesians. Non-Austronesians also inhabited the island. The early social structure of the differing groups centered on clans—small communities based on family relationships. A king called a *liurai* ruled each grouping of clans. Within a liurai's kingdom, administrative divisions known as *sucos* consisted of one prominent clan. The suco's leader obeyed the king and made payments to him in goods or services but otherwise managed the trade and social affairs of the suco without interference.

The variety of peoples and cultures in East Timor was quite complex for an island of its size. Each of East Timor's 15 ethnolinguistic groups, with its own language and culture, maintained many distinctive traits. But family resemblances and cultural similarities among the island's peoples demonstrate that tribal alliances, trade networks, social outings, and traditional gift giving strengthened political ties and fostered unity.

For many centuries, the peoples of Timor avoided the influence of foreign powers. This was partly because major commercial routes ran north of Timor Island. Nevertheless, Chinese, Malay, and Arab traders periodically landed. They negotiated with the Timorese to buy goods but were not allowed to settle or to explore inland. Although large Hindu and Buddhist empires had arisen in the archipelago, by the fifteenth century, Arab missionaries had converted most of the islanders in the region to Islam. Yet Timor still avoided the area's major religious and cultural transformation.

THE PORTUGUESE ARRIVE

In the early sixteenth century, the Portuguese began trading directly with Southeast Asia. In addition to fostering commerce in the area, the Portuguese saw an opportunity to spread their Roman Catholic religion.

During the early 1500s, the Portuguese tried to capture much of the trade in cloves and other spices grown on the Spice Islands, which lay not far from Timor. In 1520 the Portuguese set up a landing point at Lifau on the northern coast of Timor. Lifau was not a permanent Portuguese settlement but a rest stop for merchant ships. Portuguese vessels calling at Lifau on their way to Malacca (also spelled Melaka), Macao in

Perhaps the reason for Timorese control of the island's trade while the rest of the archipelago yielded to foreign colonizers was that the Timorese coastal tribes strictly forbade foreign settlement and had a reputation for enforcing their policy by beheading any trespasser.

southern China, or back to Portugal might take on sandalwood, water, and food.

The Portuguese established the area's first large European settlement on the nearby island of Solor in 1566. The settlement originally served as a stronghold for Portuguese missionaries, who worked to convert people of neighboring islands to Christianity. Portuguese troops protected the missionaries when rival Muslim traders and their armed parties came to the area.

Over time the Portuguese soldiers, sailors, and merchants intermarried with the native peoples of the region's islands. Their descendants became known as the Topasses. They spoke Portuguese, practiced Christianity, and accompanied Portuguese trading parties to Timor where they translated for the Europeans and helped negotiate for sandalwood.

Meanwhile, in 1640 the Topasses founded a settlement on Timor at Lifau, the hub of the sandalwood trade. Over time the Topass influence on the island grew so strong that, when the Portuguese tried to establish settlements on Timor in 1702, they faced armed Topass resistance. The Portuguese maintained a second post at Lifau, alongside the Topasses, and hung on there for more than 60 years, despite repeated efforts to dislodge the settlement.

Courtesy of James Ford Bell Library, University of Minnesota

Trade negotiations with Javanese island rulers (above) *soon enabled the Dutch to gain control of islands that would become Indonesia, displacing many Portuguese living there to Larantuka.*

The Topasses called themselves Larantuqeiros, which comes from Larantuka, the name of a town on Flores Island. In the 1590s, many the Topass merchants moved to Larantuka because they couldn't get along with the Portuguese Catholic missionaries on the island of Solor. Larantuka grew and prospered, and eventually became a refuge for Portuguese people who fled from settlements throughout the archipelago that fell one-by-one to the Dutch.

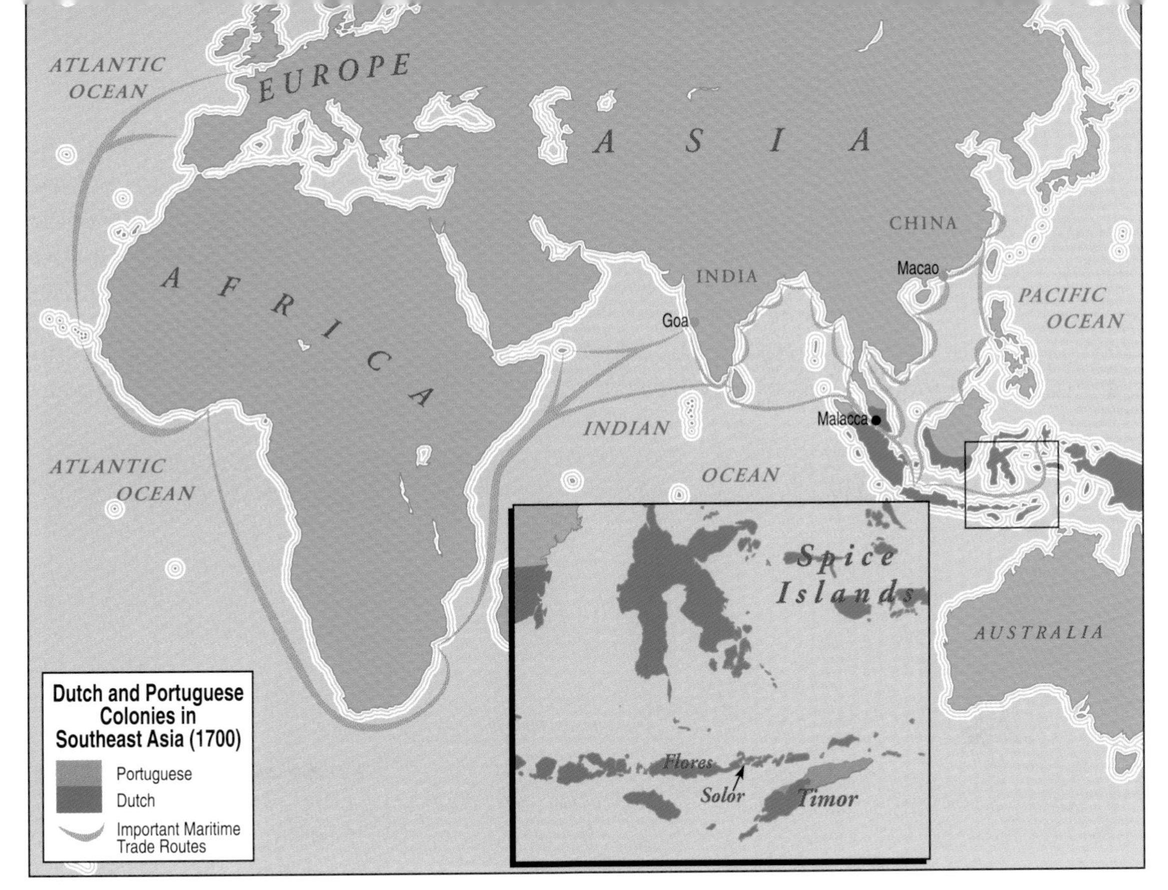

Southeast Asia's sandalwood and spice trade attracted merchants from around the world. In the 1500s, European traders established settlements, where they could rest and replenish their supplies. These settlements later became colonies.

VYING FOR CONTROL

Life was hard for the Portuguese at Lifau. They constantly had to defend themselves against sieges by their Topass neighbors. In 1769, after being under siege for almost two years, the Portuguese commander pulled out, moving his garrison east to Dili. The settlement of Dili marks the founding of the first strong, long-term Portuguese **enclave** on Timor. But by relocating, the Portuguese removed themselves from the mainstream of the sandalwood trade.

By the late 1700s, the Dutch claimed western Timor, and the Portuguese declared East Timor as theirs. Real power throughout the island, however, remained in the hands of the Topasses and the Timorese kings. The Portuguese occasionally attempted to collect taxes from the liurais of East Timor, but rebellion after rebellion weakened Portuguese authority. In addition, the closest Portuguese administrative center was located in distant Macao, so Portuguese power was further limited.

Europe's Napoleonic Wars (1792–1815) drew Dutch

and Portuguese attention away from their Timorese colonies, which then fell into neglect. A visitor to the area described Dili as "squalid, demoralized, and in a state of half-siege." The Portuguese government did nothing to encourage agricultural or economic development in the area.

"The Portuguese government of Timor is a most miserable one. Nobody seems to care the least about the improvement of the country. . . ."

Lord Alfred Wallace, author and naturalist

By the late nineteenth century, the Portuguese realized that, to maintain the colony, East Timor had to produce something profitable for export. The sandalwood heartland lay to the west in Dutch territory, and most of the trees had already been cut down anyway. Inland from the Dili coast, the Portuguese found highlands suitable for growing coffee, which soon became East Timor's main export. To cultivate coffee on land that the liurais controlled—and to cut roads through the bush to the coffee plantations—the Portuguese had to put down local rebellions. The various indigenous groups resented not only the intrusion on their land but also a tax that could usually only be paid by working for the Portuguese. The largest rebellion took place in 1896 in the Samé district in the south. Only when troops arrived from Macao in 1912 were the Portuguese able to squelch what came to be called the Great Rebellion.

The Portuguese colony finally got permission to set up an administration on Timor. In 1913 Portuguese officials signed a boundary agreement with the Dutch. In East Timor, the outnumbered Portuguese allowed traditional rulers much power. At the same time the Portuguese encouraged conflicts between kingdoms to keep them from uniting to oppose colonial rule.

Through the early twentieth century, Portuguese influence remained minimal. The Portuguese set up Catholic churches in the towns, baptized any Timorese who wanted to convert, and conducted official business in Portuguese. They did not, however, aggressively push Catholicism onto local peoples or demand the extinction of local languages or religions. The result of this relaxed approach was that church membership was not particularly large, and Portuguese was not widely spoken.

In 1926 Antonio Salazar, an authoritarian politician, came to power in Portugal. All of Portugal's colonies, including East Timor, experienced the effects of his strict and dictatorial leadership. Under new legislation the local colonial populations had to absorb Portuguese culture—this included speaking Portuguese, converting to Catholicism, and adopting Portuguese styles of dress—in order to reap colonial benefits. These benefits included the right to vote, and access to employment and education. Many people were unable to meet the standards the Portuguese set, so illiteracy in Portuguese was high, and forced labor was common.

WORLD WAR II

East Timor, one of Portugal's poorest and most distant possessions, slipped into sleepy neglect. Few other nations took notice. But this neglect changed in the 1930s, when Japan began attacking China. By the early 1940s, Japan was making lightning progress through Southeast Asia, and World War II (1939–1945) was well under way. As a result, virtually unknown islands such as East Timor took on enormous significance for the Allies (the nations fighting Japan and other enemy countries). Australia, a key ally in the Pacific theater of war, faced Japanese conquest, so Timor and other nearby islands became strategically important as the Allies planned their defense of the area.

Many of the Portuguese colonial officials on Timor in 1942 privately opposed Japan's march of conquest but lacked the military power to stop it. Consequently, the responsibility for resisting Japanese occupation of Timor fell to the Allied nations closest to the problem—Australia and the colonial power in most of the archipelago, the Netherlands. In 1942 the Japanese attacked and occupied Timor. With the enthusiastic support of the East Timorese, Sparrow Force, an Australian commando unit, waged guerrilla war against the Japanese.

After the Australian forces were evacuated, Japanese forces remained on Timor throughout the war. When the Japanese surrendered to the Allies in 1945, western Timor returned to the Dutch, and eastern Timor returned to the Portuguese. Most of the cities and towns on the island, which had been targeted by Allied bombers from northern Australia, were in ruins.

Courtesy of National Archives

The Japanese bombed the Chinese city of Shanghai shortly before the start of World War II. Japanese troops advanced rapidly through Southeast Asia, eventually occupying most of the islands, including Timor, by 1942.

Sparrow Force

The Japanese began bombing Timor in January 1942. By then Australian commandos in a group called Sparrow Force had been in Timor for about a month, learning the territory and establishing contacts among the Timorese. Most of the 1,200 Australian commandos had dug in with the Dutch forces near Kupang in West Timor—the most likely point of invasion for the Japanese—but a few had gone east to Dili. In February 1942, a Japanese force totally overwhelmed an Australian contingent near Kupang. Some of the surviving Australians fled to East Timor to join up with the Sparrow Force commandos in Dili.

The decision to operate from East Timor proved beneficial for the commandos. In the west, the leaders of the Atoni kingdoms cooperated with the Japanese against Australian and Dutch guerrillas. In the east, the Tetum and Mambai leaders took the opposite position, helping the Australians and the Dutch fight the Japanese. The Australian commandos and their East Timorese allies launched occasional attacks against Japanese positions, but their greater value was as sources of military intelligence. Information supplied by the East Timorese enabled Allied bombers based in Darwin, Australia, to cause significant damage to Japanese equipment in East Timor.

Damien Parer, Australian War Memorial Archive, Negative Number .013979

An East Timorese crew helps members of Australia's Sparrow Force construct a hut.

The resident commandos, who had been in East Timor long enough to learn Tetum, were evacuated to Australia after Japanese reinforcements landed in East Timor in late 1942. Most of the East Timorese were not so lucky. They had nowhere to go and were severely punished by Japanese forces intent on vengeance. Villages suspected of having harbored Sparrow Force were burned down, and all livestock and crops were destroyed. The number of Timorese from both parts of the island who died in the war is probably around 40,000. Many lost their lives from starvation because the Japanese commandeered much of the island's food supply.

THE POSTWAR YEARS

At the end of World War II, Indonesia gained independence, and in 1949 the Republic of Indonesia became the internationally recognized successor state to the Netherlands East Indies. As such, it took undisputed possession of all former Dutch holdings in the region (except the western end of the island of New Guinea, which the Dutch retained until the early 1960s).The Indonesian territory did not include East Timor, which had never been a Dutch possession and remained under Portuguese control.

Unlike Indonesia, East Timor had no strong independence movement. The Portuguese quickly squelched a short-lived rebellion in 1959. But it was unclear whether the rebellion's goal was to integrate East Timor with Indonesia or to support rebels in the nearby South Moluccas who wanted to break away from Indonesia.

In the postwar years, **anti-colonialism** was in the air worldwide, and resolutions decrying colonialism became commonplace at UN meetings. In response, Portugal changed East Timor's status

The Pancasila

At the end of World War II, the leaders of Indonesia's independence movement hoped to unite thousands of scattered islands in the Indonesian archipelago into a new nation. They believed that one important unifying tool would be a set of national principles on which Indonesian society would be built.

In 1945 Sukarno (a leader of the independence movement) set out five basic ideas, known collectively as the Pancasila—the Five Principles. The name was chosen to heighten their importance. For example, *panca* is an old, classical word for the number five. The everyday word used by most Indonesians is *lima*. The elements of the Pancasila are belief in God, human unity, Indonesian nationalism, representative government, and social justice.

A coat of arms used on official Indonesian documents and government property symbolically depicts these principles. Inside a shield on an eagle's breast, God is represented by a star, human unity by a circular chain, nationalism by a bull's head, representative government by a many-trunked banyan tree, and social justice by sprigs of cotton and wheat.

Associated Press Photo

Otelo Saraiva de Carvalho, an engineer of the 1974 coup in Portugal, raises his arms in victory. In his hand he holds a carnation—a symbol of the coup that came to be called the Carnation Revolution. Soldiers had put flowers in the barrels of their guns to show that no blood would be spilled.

from a colony to an overseas province, an action that technically granted the territory the same status as any part of mainland Portugal. The UN did not accept the change, however, labeling East Timor a non–self-governing (or not independent) territory. Whether or not East Timor was a colony or a province, Portugal's right to administer it went unquestioned. Later UN resolutions urged Portugal to let the East Timorese determine their own status, but Portugal never conducted a public vote in East Timor on the subject. In the 1960s, partly in response to international criticism, Portugal allowed the Timorese to hold some administrative positions in the government and began sponsoring the higher education of limited numbers of young East Timorese.

In Portugal itself, change was also in the air. Salazar died in 1970, and his successor was clashing with reformers. In 1974 officers from the Portuguese armed forces conducted a bloodless coup that removed Salazar's successor from office. Many of the coup's leaders had strong anticolonial beliefs and thought that Portugal should spend less of its resources controlling its foreign possessions and more on making reforms at home. The new Portuguese government made many reforms, including ratifying legislation that permitted people in the colonies to form political associations. The laws boosted independence movements in Portuguese colonies, and by 1975 all of Portugal's African colonies had gained independence.

The Portuguese government remained on the sidelines, following a policy of *apartidarismo*—that is, it refused to take sides in the political struggles in its present or former colonies. Portugal had acknowledged the right of its colonies to become independent and had little interest in spending limited funds to influence faraway events.

POLITICAL ASSOCIATIONS

The East Timorese caught the whiff of change as soon as they heard of Portugal's bloodless revolution. East Timor's Portuguese governor, Colonel Alves Aldeia, announced that the East Timorese were free to establish political unions. Groups formed, each with a different stance on the future of East Timor. But with no official Timorese government set up, they were powerless to take action.

One of the first political groups to emerge was the UDT. The UDT favored independence from Portugal but only after a period of gradual transition to local rule. The group felt that economic support from foreign investors would keep East Timor on its feet after Portugal pulled out. This conservative position was supported by most of East Timor's Chinese businesspeople, by small-scale farmers, and by others who felt that sudden change would do more harm than good. The UDT's middle-class leaders, including Mário Carrascalão and his brother João Carrascalão, generally had some administrative experience under the Portuguese.

João Carrascalão is one of the founding members of the UDT. His party's goal was to achieve gradual independence from Portugal.

Small parties formed in East Timor after the revolution in Portugal. A coalition of seven mountain chiefs, who claimed to be descended from the Topasses, formed Klibur Oan Timor Aswain (KOTA). The party advocated restoring rule to local chiefs. Another party was the Partido Trabalhista (Labor Party), which probably had fewer than 20 members. Another tiny party—Associação Democratica Integração Timor-Leste Australia (Adlita)—advocated integrating with Australia. None of these miniparties had much real influence.

The Associação Social Democratica Timorense (ASDT) was also founded. Its aim was to obtain outright independence for the Timorese as soon as possible.

Many of the party's founders were young and urban, although inhabitants of mountain villages—from which several ASDT members had come—also supported the party. Educated by Jesuits (a Roman Catholic religious order), some ASDT members had been influenced by the social activism of the Catholic Church during the 1970s. Unlike the UDT, the ASDT platform asserted that East Timor could survive independently—without foreign investment—on an economy based upon cooperative agriculture, public health and education programs, and some international aid.

Despite having different visions for East Timor, the background of many members of the UDT was not terribly dissimilar from that of members of Fretilin. The Fretilin members were more interested in Timorese culture than were their UDT counterparts, but the two parties did not represent vastly different segments of East Timorese society.

Leading ASDT members—such as José Ramos-Horta, Xavier do Amaral, Xanana Gusmão, and Mari Alkatiri—had visited former Portuguese colonies such as Mozambique and Angola in Africa to witness successful liberation movements. Even though many of the group's leaders denied any connection to Communism, the group's rhetoric had leftist leanings. This leftist bent was reinforced when the ASDT changed its name to Revolutionary Front for an Independent East Timor (Fretilin). Not only did the new name mention revolution, but it also sounded like Frelimo, the name of the leftist party that had taken control in Mozambique.

The only other party of any size was the integrationist party Apodeti. This group advocated union with Indonesia as the only way for East Timor to thrive economically. But Apodeti recommended unification on the condition that East Timor would retain a large amount of local autonomy and that a one- to two-year transition period would precede full integration. Plantation owners, some Muslims in Dili, and traditional leaders of various kingdoms near the border with West Timor supported Apodeti. A major obstacle in the party's ability to win broad-based popular support was the criminal reputations of some party members.

Indonesia viewed most of the new parties with skepticism. The official Indonesian radio station in Kupang, West Timor, for example, routinely presented the UDT as fascist (dictatorial and highly regimented) and Fretilin as Communist. Apodeti, however, escaped Indonesia's scorn. Reports suggested that Indonesia secretly provided combat training for young Apodeti fighters.

CHOOSING SIDES

As Portugal's reformers took a more liberal course, and as Fretilin gained popularity in East Timor, Indonesia's staunchly anti-Communist government began to fear the possibility of a Communist government in East Timor. In private discussions with Australian and Portuguese officials, Indonesia tested the waters: How would the world react if Portuguese Timor became part of In-

Independent Picture Service

In 1974 Gough Whitlam, Australia's prime minister (1972–1975), supported Indonesia's move to annex East Timor on the condition that the East Timorese agree to the arrangement.

donesia? Australia's prime minister reportedly suggested that a voluntary union with Indonesia might be the best thing for East Timor. Portuguese officials indicated that Portugal would not oppose East Timor's integration into Indonesia—if that was what the East Timorese wanted. Suharto's government took the responses as signals that international reaction against an Indonesian takeover of East Timor would be mild.

Indonesia worked secretly to prepare for the annexation. An Indonesian government plan called Operasi Komodo focused on building broader support for the pro-integrationists. Reports suggested that Indonesia had already launched a military buildup in West Timor and had improved roads so troops could move more quickly to the border from Kupang.

By January 1975, the UDT and Fretilin had joined forces, offering East Timor a governing coalition, which was supported by a majority of the local population. However, as these two pro-independence parties tried to find a working relationship, they pursued different sources of support.

Fretilin's greatest asset, which the UDT envied, was support in the countryside and among villagers who had recently moved to the larger towns to find work. This support was based on common bonds shared by Fretilin leaders and the East Timorese people, including family ties and similar mountain-country roots. More important, the Fretilin party became popular among the people by conducting a variety of social-improvement programs. They set up literacy programs to teach villagers how to read in Tetum, helped new arrivals in the cities adjust to the urban environment, and encouraged people to take part in local decision making.

The UDT, on the other hand, had no similar links with the average East Timorese. Its support came from the small, conservative middle class, who wanted independence but who also wanted a more hands-off,

Oliver Strewe

In mid-1975, broad-based support for Fretilin and independence was already visibly strong. Traditionally dressed supporters (left) *rallied in the mountain town of Maubisse with Fretilin flags, while a crowd in the district of Ocussi* (below) *came out in full force to display homemade banners.*

Helen Hill

open-market economy than Fretilin proposed.

The uneasy UDT-Fretilin alliance didn't stop the coalition from attending the first meeting of a Decolonization Commission in Dili in early March 1975. The Portuguese parliament had organized the commission to set the conditions of the colonial power's withdrawal from Timor. When the commission suggested inviting Apodeti, the UDT-Fretilin coalition strongly objected. But commission leaders later met with Apodeti to invite the party to attend the next round of talks.

Soon after the Decolonization Commission met, the UDT began experiencing an internal rift, as more conservative members opposed Fretilin's liberal platform. Tensions mounted within the coalition, especially when some of the UDT's top leaders were invited to Jakarta to discuss concerns over Fretilin's leftist agenda. In May 1975, the coalition of pro-independence parties broke apart.

When the Decolonization Commission got together in June, the UDT and Apodeti sat at the table with Portuguese representatives. Fretilin boycotted the event, claiming that Apodeti represented Indonesian interests and not those of the East Timorese. Although Fretilin's decision further damaged its credibility with the UDT, Fretilin's influence and popularity among the East Timorese remained strong.

CIVIL WAR ERUPTS

The UDT-Fretilin rift worsened in July 1975, after Indonesian authorities hinted that Fretilin had planned a coup to seize power from Portugal. The Indonesians implied that the UDT should beat them to the punch. In the early hours of August 11, 1975, the UDT made its move. UDT members arrested the Portuguese chief of police and pressured police officers to supply additional arms and personnel. They took over the Dili airport and radio station, posted armed street patrols throughout the capital, declared a curfew, and demanded that all Communists be expelled from Portuguese Timor.

The UDT's forces included many police officers bearing weapons flown in from other cities in East Timor and from the colonial army in the town of Lospalos, whose captain sided with the UDT. But other garrisons of the colonial army included large numbers of Timorese conscripts who sympathized with Fretilin. These forces declared Fretilin alliance, and the heavily armed fighters took Dili. In the countryside, UDT members attacked Fretilin members, many of whom were executed, while Fretilin's newly formed military arm, called Falintil, retaliated with equal violence. Fretilin often used torture as a way of dealing with political opponents. Throughout years of fighting, there was little distinction between Fretilin and Falintil, with

In the countryside, UDT members attacked Fretilin members, many of whom were executed, while Fretilin's newly formed military arm retaliated with equal violence.

some members serving in both groups.

On August 12, the Portuguese government evacuated families of officials and tourists to Australia. Two weeks later, Mário Lemos Pires, governor of East Timor, moved the seat of Portuguese government from Dili to the Timorese island of Ataúro. By mid-September, Fretilin forces gained control of Dili and virtually all the territory east and south of the capital. Baucau, which had been a UDT stronghold early in the conflict, surrendered to Fretilin with little bloodshed.

Rumors circulated that Indonesia, which officially remained neutral during the civil war, sent soldiers as so-called volunteers to aid the UDT. For a while, UDT-led forces, aided by several hundred Indonesian volunteers, controlled western towns near the border of West Timor. But the troops couldn't hold on. By the end of September, all the UDT leaders had either evacuated to Australia, had been killed or captured by Fretilin, or had fled to West Timor.

> *"One important fact about [the] UDT is that it never advocated integration with the Republic of Indonesia."*
>
> José Ramos-Horta

Penny Tweedie

In 1975 well-armed Fretilin troops advanced on the UDT's troops. Batugadé and other towns along the East-West Timor border, which were once controlled by UDT forces, soon fell to Fretilin in mid-September. UDT troops fled into Indonesian-owned West Timor.

A FRETILIN DECLARATION

Because the Portuguese colonial government had left East Timor, Fretilin organized food distribution, police functions, and other essential services from Dili. Fretilin wanted control of East Timor but knew that it would face objection from Indonesia if it attempted to take over East Timor illegally. So Fretilin leaders were careful to state that Fretilin still recognized Portugal as the official government and was not seeking a Portuguese overthrow.

The civil war continued. The UDT, which had never been a pro-integration party, grew dependent on Indonesian support. Indonesia, having the upper hand, offered to help the UDT on the condition that it petition Presi-

Michael Richardson, *The Age*

Fretilin leaders saw their hold on East Timor slipping. On November 28, 1975, they declared the territory independent in the hope of preventing an Indonesian invasion.

dent Suharto for integration. The UDT leaders felt they had no choice but to accept the offer. Indonesia built up troops and weapons along the border and arranged for Apodeti and the UDT to work together. Although Indonesia's involvement wasn't yet formally recognized, the UDT-Apodeti coalition had Indonesian equipment and included Indonesian volunteers.

The anti-Fretilin counterattack began in October. Town after town fell to the Indonesian-backed UDT-Apodeti troops. Atabae—one of Fretilin's last strongholds near the West Timor border—fell on November 26. The defeat of this town forced Fretilin's leaders to ask for international support as a way to prevent a full-scale Indonesian invasion. In a hastily organized ceremony in Dili on November 28, Fretilin's leadership declared East Timor a free and independent nation to be known as the Democratic Republic of East Timor. Only four countries—all former Portuguese colonies—recognized the newly declared state. In response to Fretilin's action, the integration coalition—openly backed by Indonesia—disregarded Fretilin's declaration and issued its own: with the Portuguese gone, East Timor had decided to become part of Indonesia. ⊕

The Rome Memorandum

International reaction to the civil war in East Timor was mild, except in Indonesia and Portugal. The Indonesian government suggested a meeting with Portuguese officials on the condition that neither East Timor nor the UN be involved in negotiations. Ignoring repeated telegrams from East Timor's Governor Pires requesting help to restore the peace, officials in Lisbon agreed to meet with Indonesian officials in Rome. On November 3, Indonesia and Portugal issued a document known as the Rome Memorandum of Understanding. In the memorandum, Indonesia acknowledged Portugal as East Timor's administering authority and urged the Portuguese to end the fighting. Portugal conceded Indonesia's strategic interest in East Timor. Fretilin refused to acknowledge the memorandum.

CHAPTER

3

THE PRESENT CONFLICT

Indonesia conducted a full-scale invasion of East Timor on Sunday, December 7, 1975. In the pre-dawn hours, Indonesian gunships anchored off Dili shelled the town, while bombers attacked Fretilin gun emplacements. In other parts of the capital, about 3,000 troops took positions on the ground. They met resistance from Fretilin fighters, but part of the action that day was against unarmed civilians whom the soldiers believed to be Fretilin supporters.

Troops turned Dili inside out, looting the city of valuables. Soldiers vandalized property and executed unarmed civilians. Some raped or kidnapped Timorese women. According to reports by Amnesty International (an independent organization that works to ensure basic human rights), Indonesian forces singled out for execution Dili's Chinese citizens—reports not hard to believe in light of Indonesia's anti-Chinese laws at that time. About 2,000 East Timorese, mostly civilians, were killed in the initial invasion.

Indonesian soldiers had secretly been aiding the UDT troops for months. On December 7, 1975, when Indonesian soldiers landed on East Timor's beaches (left) *and advanced on Dili, Indonesia became officially involved in East Timor's affairs.* Facing page: *The territory of East Timor is dwarfed by Indonesia. Although the governments of nearby countries have chosen to stay out of Indonesia's affairs, students and organizations have spoken out against Indonesia's occupation of East Timor.*

JAKARTA Capital
Darwin Major City
International Border
MALAYSIA Country Name
IRYAN JAYA Province Name
THAILAND
CAMBODIA
VIETNAM
PHILIPPINES
SOUTH PACIFIC OCEAN
Malay Peninsula
MALAYSIA
KUALA LUMPUR
Malacca (Melaka)
SINGAPORE
BRUNEI
MALAYSIA
Borneo
Sumatra
Sulawesi (Celebes)
INDONESIA
Ambon
NEW GUINEA
IRYAN JAYA
JAKARTA
Java
Bali
Flores
DILI
Solor
Timor
KUPANG
Lesser Sunda Islands
Timor Sea
PAPUA NEW GUINEA
INDIAN OCEAN
Darwin
AUSTRALIA

Indonesia sent paratroopers to aid the ground troops in combatting Fretilin forces. As Indonesia gained more ground, the East Timorese who could escape found shelter in the mountains. Those who were captured were placed in prison camps to keep them from aiding the resistance.

Troops sent most Dili residents to a prison camp just outside of town. Even pro-Indonesian commentators later described the Indonesian capture of Dili as a shameful display of poor discipline, greed, and brutality.

The big coastal towns soon came under Indonesian authority, but Fretilin continued to control the East Timorese interior. International reaction against the invasion was stronger than Indonesia had expected. On December 8, the dispossessed Portuguese administration of Governor Lemos Pires fled to Australia, ending Portuguese rule. Portugal broke diplomatic ties with Indonesia on December 10. The UN passed a resolution on December 12, condemning the invasion and demanding Indonesia's withdrawal from East Timor. On December 22, the UN told Indonesia to remove its troops. The United States reacted angrily to the degree of violence but didn't threaten retaliation.

With Portuguese influence effectively terminated, Indonesia moved quickly to create a provisional government, with Apodeti's leader, Arnaldo dos Reis Araújo, as governor. The Indonesians, reasoning that Portugal had abandoned the territory, established a People's Representative Council in Dili. In June 1976, this council—made up of members of the UDT-Apodeti coalition—requested that East Timor be allowed to join the Republic of Indonesia. Within days the Indonesian government announced that it would grant the request, and the merger formally took effect in August 1976.

Indonesia initially faced harsh international criticism. But armed with a rationale for intervention based on Portugal's abandonment and the council's request for union, Suharto's government seemed willing to weather the criticism and to let time dull international memory.

CLOSING THE DOOR

By the end of 1976, Indonesia had 30,000 soldiers in East Timor. But Fretilin hadn't given up. It had stockpiled food and other supplies in the back country and remained in control of 80 percent of East Timorese territory. Crops and food reserves supported hundreds of thousands of fleeing civilians as well as the members of Fretilin. Indonesia wanted to adopt tougher tactics to counter Fretilin's guerrilla war but had to find a way to do so without attracting further international notice.

To accomplish this goal, Indonesia closed off East Timor from public view. After 1976 Indonesian officials carefully controlled what diplomats, UN representatives, and other foreign visitors were allowed to see. The Indonesians steered them away from controversial spots such as combat zones and resettlement (prison) camps. The Indonesian authorities also regulated the news coming out of the territory. The official story was that the East Timorese welcomed Indonesian protection from Fretilin terrorists, that guerrilla resistance had

Before and during the invasion of East Timor, several foreign correspondents were killed by Indonesian soldiers or their Timorese allies. In the battle for Balibo in October 1975, five journalists from Australian television stations disappeared. Eyewitnesses later reported that Indonesian-UDT forces had killed the journalists and then placed their bodies in a burning building. One month later, Australian journalist Roger East—the only foreign correspondent left in town—was executed in the invasion of Dili.

AP Radio Photo

The Australian flag adorning a building in Dili stood as a memorial to the journalists killed there.

almost vanished, and that life was improving dramatically for the populace.

This picture contrasted greatly with the one painted by rare visitors to the territory and by the East Timorese who had managed to escape, to broadcast illegal radio messages to Australia, or to smuggle out notes. These unofficial accounts told of a still-strong anti-Indonesian resistance in the rugged interior and of Indonesian brutality.

Much about East Timor during these hazy years remains in dispute, but one certainty is that many East Timorese died in a very short time. In 1976 Francisco Lopes da Cruz, a member of the Indonesian-installed gov-

Resettlement Camps

Many of the East Timorese, who were driven out of the back country and from rural areas, were confined to Indonesian resettlement camps. There, the Indonesians thought, they could more easily prevent the local populace from aiding the Fretilin guerrillas. But strong political and social ties in resettlement camps and in rural areas helped maintain the network of organized resistance, enabling Fretilin to remain a strong, but illusive force.

In the camps, the East Timorese were pressed into forced-labor crews but rarely were provided enough food, and medical care was almost nonexistent. The few international visitors who saw camps reported severe malnutrition, rampant malaria, and other diseases.

Peter Rodgers

During the invasion, many people were forced from the mountains into resettlement camps, where food and medical supplies were scarce.

Penny Tweedie/Panos Pictures

Left: *Women were active in defending Timorese-controlled territory.* Below: *Indonesian troops destroyed homes and burned crops, forcing many families from their lands.*

ernment and a former UDT leader, announced that 60,000 East Timorese—about a tenth of the population—had died in the first months of the civil war. International suspicions arose. If the government admitted these large numbers, observers reasoned, the real toll might be much higher. Unofficial reports stated that the death toll was closer to 100,000.

Fretilin had executed at least 150 and perhaps as many as 1,000 prisoners just after the Indonesian invasion. Most Fretilin victims were UDT and Apodeti members. Fretilin killed many more East Timorese, especially suspected collaborators with Indonesia, during the next few years. But most deaths in East Timor were not conventional battlefield casualties. It is likely that Indonesian violence against the civilian population caused the majority of the casualties.

UNUSUAL TACTICS

Between 1977 and 1979, Indonesian forces employed a tactic known as encirclement and annihilation. The military would surround an area and then unleash an aerial attack. Afterward ground troops would lay waste to the encircled areas, killing anyone they came across and destroying villages and farms. Indonesian aircraft—including planes

Fretilin remained faithful to its mission to provide education and services to the East Timorese. In mountain refuges, instructors found time to give lessons in Tetum.

bought from the United States—also dropped toxic chemicals across the land, killing crops and trees and poisoning the water. Some foreign newspapers reported strikes with napalm, a chemical that catches fire as it hits its target. As civilians fled these devastated areas, Indonesian troops arrested them and tried to extract from them information about Fretilin military positions. Torture and public executions were common interrogation techniques.

One of many Indonesian encirclement and annihilation campaigns took place in late 1978 on Mount Matebian, one of the last Fretilin strongholds and a refuge for large groups of East Timorese civilians. Located near the town of Quelicai in the eastern part of the territory, Mount Matebian supported crops, provided shelter, and came to symbolize the Timorese will to survive. Timorese control of Mount Matebian was especially meaningful to the people because *matebian* means "soul" in Tetum.

Because of the mountain's symbolic value, Indonesian troops, who were growing increasingly frustrated with Fretilin resistance, were particularly thorough in their efforts to drive civilians from the mountain. In a new form of execution, Indonesian pilots took Timorese prisoners up in helicopters and threw them into the ocean below. This method was called *mandi laut* or "going for a swim in the sea." Indonesian soldiers eventually drove all Timorese civilians and guerrillas from Mount Matebian, dealing Fretilin a severe psychological blow.

Civilians who had managed to escape the Indonesians fled to the mountains, where Fretilin remained in control. Among the refugees were Catholic priests. Within these small mountain communities, a new relationship formed between the Catholic clergy and the East Timorese—one of mutual trust and shared fear of a common enemy.

Ross Bird

Each year people return to Mount Matebian to mourn and remember their loved ones killed in the 1978 attack on the mountain.

Fence of Legs

In 1981 about 80,000 East Timorese boys and men were forced to walk side by side across the territory in a "fence of legs" operation to snare hiding Fretilin guerrillas. One line of marchers was arrayed from north to south across the island near the eastern end, and another line was positioned in the same fashion near the border with West Timor. The first line marched west toward the center of East Timor, while the second line marched east toward the same spot. The Indonesians hoped to sweep the guerrillas toward an easy catchpoint in the middle. Indonesian troops marched with the lines of civilians. The operation failed, however, because of both the Timorese unwillingness to betray the guerrillas and the island's rough terrain. The fence of legs passed right through Fretilin territory without dislodging many guerrillas.

Civilian victims of the "fence of legs" operation

Xanana Gusmão

Enny Nuraheni/Reuters/Archive Photos

The name Kay Rala Xanana Gusmão—or usually just Xanana—has become a rallying cry at anti-Indonesian protests throughout East Timor. It is the guerrilla nickname of José Alexandre Gusmão, the figurehead of the East Timorese resistance movement.

Gusmão's father was a schoolmaster who also worked part-time in a cheese factory. The family was "*civilizado*"—a Portuguese term for East Timorese who had become civilized in the ways of the Portuguese. Young José was sent to the Catholic seminary high school at Daré near Dili, but he didn't want to become a priest. After dropping out of the seminary, he got jobs first as a typist for the government's health service and then repairing electrical appliances.

Gusmão was one of the early founders of Fretilin, and in 1975 took to the hills. There he studied the work of the Chinese Communist leader Mao Ze-dong and became serious about politics.

Gusmão's rise to the leadership of Fretilin was slow, and in 1981 he assumed the job reluctantly. But he succeeded in revitalizing an almost-dead movement because of his willingness to seek broad consensus and to avoid violent revenge against opponents. It was his idea to bring diverse opponents of Indonesian occupation into a united council, even if this meant reducing Fretilin's influence. He remained the political backbone of the resistance until his arrest by Indonesian soldiers in May 1992.

Xanana spends much of his time writing and receiving visitors in his jail cell in Indonesia. Despite being in prison for a very long time, he continues to inspire the East Timorese resistance movement.

CHANGING ALIGNMENTS

Meanwhile, Fretilin leadership was losing some key members. Two of its founders, José Ramos-Horta and Mari Alkatiri, were abroad advocating the party's cause and were largely unable to communicate with Fretilin leaders in the mountains. In East Timor, leaders fell in battle, surrendered, or were arrested by Indonesian forces. In addition, the East Timorese resistance was no longer an all-Fretilin affair. After witnessing Indonesian brutality to the Timorese, some members of Apodeti and the UDT were beginning to oppose the very occupation they had helped to bring about.

In 1981 a long-time Fretilin member, Xanana Gusmão, took over the presidency of Fretilin. The party began to reach out to other resistance groups in ways that would have been unthinkable before party alignments began to shift. Fretilin became part of a wider umbrella organization called the Revolutionary Council of National Resistance (renamed the National Council for Maubere Resistance—CNRM—in 1986). The council united several opponents of the In-

Cease-fire Attempt

The encirclement programs had crippled Fretilin's forces. However, the strong network of organized resistance in East Timor helped get Fretilin back on its feet. By 1983 Fretilin fighters were conducting a successful guerrilla war against Indonesian troops.

In the face of this renewed resistance, Indonesian commanders began negotiations for a cease-fire. On March 21, three Indonesian military officials met with a Fretilin delegation. After a second set of talks, both parties signed a cease-fire agreement on June 25.

The Australian government at the time was strongly against Indonesia's occupation of East Timor. To regain Australia's support, Indonesian officials portrayed the cease-fire as a gesture of good will to the East Timorese. The Indonesian government agreed to host a tour of East Timor to an Australian delegation. Outwardly the delegation was on a fact-finding mission to examine the effects of Indonesian occupation. But Indonesia also hoped to rebuild its soured relations with Australia.

The Australian delegation spent four of their ten days in East Timor with an Indonesian military interpreter who knew the local language. They spent the rest of their visit in Indonesia. They were told that poor road conditions would prevent them from going to many of the sites in the East Timor interior. Fretlin had hoped to talk with the delegation, but the Indonesian tour guides made no such arrangements. Instead Fretilin members intercepted the Australian delegation and were greeted on less-than-friendly terms.

After the delegation left, the Australian government published positive reports of the visit. The reports confirmed Indonesia's official story that it was justified in its occupation of East Timor. This report heartened Indonesian authorities, who launched a military offensive on August 8, breaking the cease-fire agreement.

donesian occupation. The CNRM wanted to create its own image and to distinguish itself from its well-known member, Fretilin. To appease other CNRM parties, Gusmão retired from Fretilin in 1984, and the organization regrouped as the armed forces of East Timorese resistance under Gusmão.

The local leadership of the Roman Catholic Church also changed during the 1980s. Dili's Portuguese bishop, Joaquim Ribeiro, retired. In his place came Monsignor Martinho da Costa Lopes, an East Timorese priest whose appointment signaled a significant shift of authority to the local Timorese church. After speaking out against the Indonesian regime's brutality, da Costa Lopes resigned. Pope John Paul II replaced him with Monsignor Carlos Felipe Ximenes Belo, an East Timorese priest who had been studying in Rome during the Indonesian invasion. Expecting Belo to be less critical of their behavior, the Indonesians seemed pleased with his appointment.

The pope was careful, however, to minimize the Indonesian government's ability to influence church policy. Instead of making Belo the bishop of Dili, the pope made him the direct papal representative. Belo was a bishop who operated *from* Dili, but he was not the bishop *of* Dili. This technicality kept Belo out of the Indonesian Bishops' Council, an organization of Catholic bishops in Indonesia. The strategic appointment protected him from potential pressure from Indonesian colleagues on the council who might be unsympathetic to the East Timorese point of view. In addition, the move to skirt membership in the council allowed the Roman Catholic Church to avoid implying—through Belo's membership—official recognition of the Indonesian occupation of East Timor.

A NEW GENERATION OF PROTESTERS

Through the mid- and late 1980s, human-rights groups such as Amnesty International, Asia Watch, and the International Committee of the Red Cross (ICRC) continued to decry the Indonesian treatment of refugees from East Timor. These groups were joined by the Roman Catholic Church and the government of Portugal. But with little international opposition, Indonesia was left to consolidate its control over the territory.

By 1988 the government in Jakarta was feeling confident enough to open East Timor once again to outside visitors. By that time, about 200,000 East Timorese had died in the conflict. Certain areas where guerrilla activity was still frequent remained out of bounds, but most of East Timor was accessible to foreigners as of January 1989.

The feeling of openness extended into the political realm as well. In February 1989, Bishop Belo urged the UN to arrange a vote of self-determination for East Timor. Other voices from within the territory spoke out, too. Indonesia's governor in East Timor, the former UDT founder Mário Carrascalão, embarrassed his bosses in Jakarta by publicizing the fact that more than 90 percent of the East Timorese were illiterate and that more than half of them suffered from tuberculosis because of the region's inadequate health care system. This publicity was a blow to Jakarta, which had proclaimed economic development in East Timor as one rationale for Indonesia's presence there.

After Pope John Paul II announced he would visit the territory in October 1989, the Indonesian military redoubled its efforts to capture Fretilin leaders but met with no success. During the papal visit, the pope held an outdoor mass in Dili that about 100,000 people attended. After the mass, chants went up from the crowd in favor of independence and decry-

> *"I am fully aware of the norms of the Roman Catholic Church, which demands that its religious leaders refrain from [politics]. But as a bishop I have the moral duty to speak for the poor and simple people who . . . cannot defend themselves. . . . "*
>
> Bishop Belo

Demonstrators used the pope's visit as an opportunity to protest the occupation in front of Catholic officials and the international media, but they were violently dispersed by Indonesian police. Many young people are disappointed by the lack of support from church officials at an international level.

ing the Indonesian occupation. Indonesian police entered the crowd and beat protesters to break up the demonstration. The next day, a military sweep through Dili resulted in the arrest of 40 young people suspected of organizing the protest.

This episode highlighted what was to become Indonesia's biggest problem in East Timor during the 1990s—protest by a generation of young people, mainly students, who strongly resented the Indonesian occupation. While the older Fretilin guerrillas in the mountains still posed a military challenge, the restless population of Dili and other towns was drawing more international attention through demonstrations and growing media coverage. As Communist governments in Europe and Asia fell apart, it became harder for Jakarta to portray the demonstrations in East Timor as the work of a dangerous international Communist conspiracy.

Many of the young East Timorese being hunted by the Indonesian police sought

> *"The most dramatic indictment of Indonesian rule is that the youth, brought up to speak Indonesian and far better educated than had ever been the case during the Portuguese period, are perhaps the most anti-Indonesian of the entire population."*

refuge either in churches or at Bishop Belo's residence. Those who found shelter in Belo's home were left alone by security forces. But the dissidents who hid in churches fared less well and were often harassed by ninjas. Ninjas are teenagers dressed in black whom the Indonesian security forces reportedly employ to frighten ordinary East Timorese into staying home at night.

© Steve Cox

In anticipation of the Portuguese visit, protesters made anti-Indonesian signs to display at a planned demonstration. A masked East Timorese youth hides his identity for a photograph to avoid being recognized and punished for his involvement with the anti-Indonesian movement.

THE DILI MASSACRE

In 1991 young dissidents throughout East Timor were looking forward to the November arrival of a long-awaited parliamentary delegation from Portugal. For the East Timorese, the visit of the Portuguese—still recognized by most of the world as the legitimate government of East Timor—held great promise. No one expected the Portuguese to retake Dili and begin governing again, but people hoped that the visit might put the conflict higher on the world's agenda. If the Indonesians and the Portuguese talked more, perhaps a vote on East Timor's future might eventually result. At the very least, the Portuguese visit would provide an opportunity to unfurl anti-Indonesian banners in

© Steve Cox

A small group of friends and family gather to mourn the loss of Sebastião Gomes. Gomes's death precipitated events at Santa Cruz Cemetery that would bring international attention to the small territory of East Timor.

front of news cameras from Europe and North America.

On October 27, the Indonesian police crushed scattered student demonstrations in Dili. More than 30 demonstrators tried to avoid police sweeps by taking refuge in a church in the city's western suburbs. In the predawn hours of the next day, ninjas showed up at the church, and the ensuing clash drew in the police. In the end, two people lay dead—one ninja and one anti-Indonesian activist named Sebastião Gomes.

Gomes's death drew unexpected outrage from the residents of Dili, about half of whom took to the streets after daybreak to shout their anger. Another large demonstration followed on October 29. Amid this emotionally charged atmosphere came the announcement that the Portuguese delegation would not be visiting Dili after all. The plan had fallen apart because Indonesia refused to allow an Australian journalist, Jill Joliffe, to accompany the Portuguese legislators. Indonesian authorities knew that Joliffe had written reports that were highly critical of Indonesia, and at the last minute they barred her entry. The Portuguese would not bow to Joliffe's exclusion.

The combination of Gomes's death and the cancellation of Portugal's visit created enormous frustration that erupted just after sunrise on November 12. A procession started from the church where Gomes had died and wound its way toward Santa Cruz Cemetery,

The memorial group for Gomes was joined by thousands of demonstrators who filled the cemetery and stood atop the gates, displaying banners that were made for the Portuguese visit.

where he was buried. What started as a small crowd quickly grew to hundreds as people along the way joined in. Some of the marchers chanted "Long Live East Timor." At one point, a group of demonstrators met an Indonesian army officer who tried to persuade them to break up the march. Although the encounter began politely, an angry protester broke from the crowd and stabbed the officer with a knife, inflicting minor injuries.

At the cemetery, the marchers mixed with mourners who were holding a quiet memorial for Gomes. By this time, the crowd had swelled to some 3,000 people who were singing, shouting, and waving Fretilin party flags. Just as some members of the crowd started to leave the cemetery, about 60 soldiers pulled up in transport vehicles. Angered by the stabbing of the officer, the soldiers surrounded the cemetery and fired into the crowd, wounding and killing many. Those who weren't downed by gunfire rushed toward the gates. The soldiers continued their gunfire, however, and beat individuals with rifle butts and riot sticks. Other soldiers then entered the cemetery to kill any wounded that were still alive.

After the initial attack on Santa Cruz Cemetery, according to journalist Andrew MacMillan, Indonesian soldiers walked through the cemetery and killed wounded survivors they came across. Three hours after the attack ended, Governor Carrascalão's wife, Milina, went to the cemetery and found 18 seriously wounded people still lying on the ground. When she asked the military why the victims weren't taken to the hospital, the soldiers claimed there weren't enough vehicles to transport them. In the following days, the Indonesian police rounded up 80 suspected troublemakers and executed them beside a newly dug grave outside Dili.

NO END IN SIGHT

Sources disagree about the total number of casualties at Santa Cruz. A widely respected estimate published in 1992 by a Portuguese human-rights group holds that 271 people were killed, 382 were wounded, and 250 were missing. The Indonesian government—after first claiming that only 19 people had been killed and 91 wounded—eventually revised the number to 50 dead and 200 wounded. More critical than the discussion of numbers was the fact that the Dili Massacre had happened in full view of foreign observers. Journalist Max Stahl even recorded the incident on a videotape, which he managed to smuggle to Australia. After the events of November 1991, the Indonesian government could no longer credibly deny the violence in East Timor.

> *"In a developing country as large as Indonesia . . . , human rights violations, unfortunately, do occur. . . . These occurrences do not reflect the government policy; in fact, the violators were brought to justice and were given prison sentences."*
>
> Hupudio Supardi, Embassy of Indonesia

The well-publicized Dili Massacre incited worldwide opposition to the Indonesian occupation of East Timor. International television coverage of the incident often included clips from Stahl's videotape. The viewing public was also made aware that the United States, Britain, and Australia had supplied the weaponry used by Indonesia's forces in East Timor. The UN again debated the East Timor issue, eventually passing a resolution critical of Indonesia's human-rights record. The United States continued to approve sales of arms and fighter planes to Indonesia but did cut back on military aid.

The Suharto government later admitted that some Indonesian soldiers in East Timor had been involved in a "regrettable" clash with demonstrators. Spokesperson after spokesperson declared that the soldiers had been goaded into violence, pointing to the stabbing incident and to unsubstantiated claims of demonstrators lobbing grenades at the soldiers. The government put a few low-ranking military men on trial and sentenced them to prison terms of less than two years. Higher-ranking officers, who were not at the cemetery but who had responsibility for the units involved, were reprimanded or transferred to other jobs. Thirteen civilians who had taken part in the procession were also put on trial. Each was sentenced to at least 15 years in prison.

Reuters/Gary Cameron/Archive Photos

Before speaking at a press conference in Jakarta where he was attending an APEC meeting, President Clinton was assured that East Timorese demonstrators at the U.S. Embassy were in no danger. Clinton has been more willing than other U.S. presidents to voice his concerns to Suharto regarding human-rights violations in East Timor.

International outrage over the Dili Massacre didn't bring peace to East Timor, but it may have prevented the Indonesian troops from summarily executing Gusmão whom they captured in Dili in 1992. The forces held him under tight guard, put him on trial for rebellion, and in 1993 sentenced him to 20 years in Jakarta's Cipinang Prison. Gusmão is allowed frequent visitors, perhaps to allay any suspicions that he is being mistreated.

After Gusmão's capture, the leadership of Fretilin fell to a commander named Ma'Huno, Gusmão's deputy and the only one of Fretilin's founders who was still alive, still in East Timor, and still free. But in April 1993, Ma'Huno, too, was captured, and the leadership devolved to Konis Santana. Gusmão still remains the living symbol of East Timorese resistance. Ramos-Horta continued to work from abroad keeping East Timor on the world's political agenda.

Guerrilla fighting continued in the countryside during the early and mid-1990s, but Indonesia had far more trouble with urban unrest. On November 12, 1994, on the third anniversary of the Dili Massacre, widespread rioting erupted in Dili. The same day, U.S. president Bill Clinton was in Jakarta for a meeting of the Asia Pacific Economic Cooperation (APEC) forum. A group of 29 East Timorese made their way into the U.S. Embassy in Jakarta and, to a host of journalists, voiced their demands for Timorese independence and the release of Gusmão. Clinton later told President Suharto that he was concerned about human-rights violations in East Timor.

Since the Dili Massacre, Indonesia's international reputation has suffered. The awarding of the 1996 Nobel Peace Prize to Bishop Belo and Ramos-Horta raised East Timor's international profile. But it also deeply embarrassed the Indonesian government. After the prize was announced, Indonesia's foreign minister, Ali Alatas, was quick to congratulate Bishop Belo but was equally quick to denounce Ramos-Horta as a political opportunist.

The Nobel award would have embarrassed Indonesia under any circumstances. But

1996 had been a particularly bad year for Suharto's regime, which faced incidents of violence and political opposition throughout Indonesia.

In 1997 little had changed. East Timorese students continued to stage demonstrations and to get into clashes with Indonesian soldiers. The armed forces of East Timorese resistance (formerly Falintil) and the Indonesian military carried on with a small-scale guerrilla war. Ramos-Horta and Bishop Belo took advantage of their relative fame to conduct talks at UN forums and around the world. East Timor supporters in Australia, Portugal, Italy, and the United States held demonstrations in support of the East Timorese, but all to little effect.

> *"When asked how a [vote] on the issue of independence versus integration would turn out, I was told that over 90 percent of the people would choose independence. . . . "*
>
> U.S. Senator Claiborne Pell

Three-way talks among Indonesia, Portugal, and an East Timorese delegation were rescheduled several times in the hope of finding a fair solution for all parties involved. To get talks rolling, Fretilin leader Konis Santana presented a compromise solution. He stated that the rebel movement would accept a loose association with Indonesia, much like the relationship between the United States and Puerto Rico. This concession was a big step for a group that, since the Indonesian invasion, would accept nothing less than independence. But Suharto doesn't want to give any privileges to its territories for fear that other island groups will want special treatment as well, so the East Timorese continue to search for an acceptable answer.

Reuters/Enny Nuraheni/Archive Photos

After the Nobel Peace Prize was awarded to Bishop Belo and José Ramos-Horta, Suharto visited East Timor to congratulate Belo.

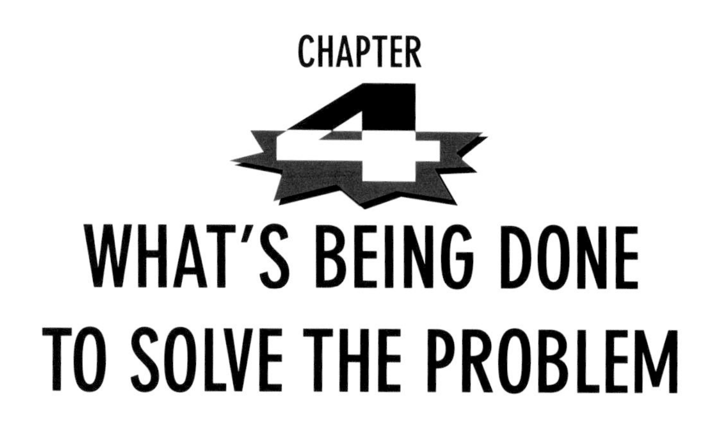

CHAPTER 4
WHAT'S BEING DONE TO SOLVE THE PROBLEM

When the Nobel Peace Prize was awarded on December 10, 1996, Bishop Carlos Felipe Ximenes Belo and José Ramos-Horta addressed a gathering of international dignitaries. In his speech, Bishop Belo cautiously called for international help in opening the dialogue to solve East Timor's problem. Ramos-Horta, on the other hand, was more explicit in his speech. He reiterated the CNRM position by urging Indonesia to release East Timorese political prisoners and further proposed a three-phase plan. First, all sides would refrain from aggression against one another. Second, East Timor would be allowed a period of autonomy, during which it would manage its own affairs without actually becoming independent. And third, the territory would hold a referendum (vote) among the East Timorese to determine the future of their territory. One or all of these ideas surfaces in nearly every proposal for a resolution in East Timor. The big question is whether change can happen.

INTERNATIONAL RELATIONS

After the 1975 invasion, the Indonesian government hoped that the world would forget about East Timor. And, in fact, few nations wanted to take action that would spoil their relations with such a geographically, culturally, religiously, and economically important nation. Indonesia borders on or contains some of the world's most important seaways, it is a major producer of oil and other important resources, and it has the world's largest Muslim population. So, by and large, the international community seemed content to criticize Indonesia's occupation without taking measures to end it.

From 1975 to 1982, the UN voted every year on Indonesia's takeover of East Timor. And each time, the organization passed a resolution condemning the occupation and calling for a vote of self-determination. In every UN vote, however, Indonesia gained a bit more support. In 1975 only nine countries sided with Indonesia. By 1982, 46 countries had taken Indonesia's side.

The Timor Gap Treaty

Countries that border a sea have certain rights to use the water and to explore and develop the resources of the underlying seabed. A set of complicated rules—known as the law of the sea—determines the physical boundaries of each nation's rights. In many cases, however, these boundaries overlap.

Australia and Indonesia, for example, had a complex, long-running dispute over rights to the Timor Sea. In some parts of this sea, the two nations agreed on their boundaries. But the Timor Gap, a rectangular swatch south of the East Timor shoreline, caused friction for many years because of the valuable deposits of oil and gas that lie beneath the seabed.

Australia had tried to negotiate the boundary with Portugal, which administered the nearby land. But for Portugal, the matter was not urgent, so it remained unresolved. In 1978, three years after Indonesia invaded East Timor, Australia decided to try a new approach to the problem. By declaring its support for Indonesia's occupation of East Timor, Australia put itself in a strong position to negotiate rights to the Timor Gap with Indonesia. The negotiations between the two nations lasted for 10 years. Finally in December 1989, the two signed an agreement known officially as the Treaty on a Zone of Cooperation between the Indonesian province of East Timor and Northern Australia. Unofficially it's called the Timor Gap Treaty. The agreement carves up the sea into three areas. The one in the middle will be jointly developed, and the two governments will split the proceeds from leasing it out to oil companies. In another zone, closer to Timor Island, Indonesia gets control but agrees to give Australia 10 percent of the fees it collects from oil operations. The third zone is under Australian control, and Indonesia will be paid 10 percent of Australia's revenues.

Courtesy of Northern Territory News

Australian foreign minister Gareth Evans, left, *and Indonesian foreign minister Ali Alatas,* right, *shake hands after signing the Timor Gap Treaty.*

The treaty is under dispute by Portugal, which has appealed to the International Court of Justice (ICJ) for a nullification of the treaty. Portugal's application to the court insists that Australia reopen negotiations with Portugal about the Timor Gap. In 1995 the ICJ refused to pass judgment on the case, citing that Indonesia doesn't fall under ICJ jurisdiction. Portugal continues to appeal the treaty.

From time to time, individual countries and international governmental organizations have expressed their objection to the occupation. A government or organization typically releases a letter to the press or to the UN that criticizes Indonesia's policy in East Timor. In another approach, during a visit to Jakarta for diplomatic reasons, a foreign ambassador might tell President Suharto that his or her government disapproves of the occupation. Yet many countries still trade with and make arms sales to Indonesia.

Still a Portuguese Territory

Portugal was not always so interested in actively campaigning for East Timor. Just after the revolution in 1974, Portugal withdrew from participating in world events. While going through major reforms, the country fell into deep economic repression, which also kept it from having much weight internationally. However, by 1986 Portugal had regained enough economic ground to join the European Community (now called the European Union, or EU).

Being a member of the EU may help Portugal exert more pressure on the Indonesian government. Instead of being one nation speaking out for East Timor, Portugal hopes to have the economic and political backing of other EU member countries. In addition to receiving support from governments in Europe, Portugal hopes to form a Portuguese-speaking commonwealth, which would include Brazil, Mozambique, Angola, and other former Portuguese colonies. These countries would also help Portugal in its fight for East Timor.

Portugal is one of the few governments to continually protest the East Timor situation. By contesting the Timor Gap Treaty, by aiding organizations that work for the East Timorese cause, and by participating in UN-sponsored talks, Portugal reminds the world that East Timor is an ongoing Portuguese concern. Nevertheless, Portugal's protests have not had much effect. Talks between the Portuguese and Indonesian governments have progressed slowly for several years, and the Timor Gap case remains unresolved.

In 1986 the UN held East Timor decolonization hearings. A member of the Japanese parliament raised his country's concerns regarding the issue.

A COZY NEIGHBORHOOD

Despite infrequent outbursts from the international community, Indonesia has little worry that its foreign affairs will suffer. Except for Papua New Guinea, every bordering Southeast Asian country sides with Indonesia on the East Timor matter. Even if public relations with the rest of the world went awry, the chances of Indonesia being punished by a blockade or embargo over the East Timor issue are small. Indonesia gets solid backing from Singapore, the Philippines, Malaysia, Brunei, Thailand, and Vietnam—fellow members of the Association of Southeast Asian Nations (ASEAN). Bolstered by strong economies and a sense of community, leaders of the ASEAN nations have agreed not to interfere in one another's human-rights policies so they can pursue their own plans for economic development. Human-rights agendas of Europe and the United States are often disregarded because they are viewed as imposed by outsiders and in conflict with Asian values.

U.S. Involvement

When the Portuguese pulled out of their colonies in 1974, the United States and the Soviet Union—two world superpowers then engaged in a political struggle—had strategic interests in the conflicts of Portugal's former possessions. Communist liberation movements took control in Angola and Mozambique, and the United States feared that as other Portuguese colonies gained independence, they could also become Communist.

On December 5, 1975, U.S. president Ford and his secretary of state Henry Kissinger met privately with President Suharto in Jakarta. On December 7, Indonesia invaded East Timor. Although no notes from that meeting have been published, it doesn't appear that President Ford issued a strong warning against an Indonesian invasion of East Timor.

Many human-rights groups object to continued U.S. military sales to Indonesia. While the United States has typically refrained from interfering in Indonesia's domestic affairs, President Clinton's administration is more willing than earlier administrations to criticize Indonesia's human-rights record in East Timor and has decreased military aid packages to Indonesia. Members of Congress have spoken out against military aid programs, but both the executive and legislative branches of the government keep approving the aid packages. The United States has long supported the Suharto regime as a stabilizing influence in heavily Muslim-populated Southeast Asia. In addition, American submarines require passage through two deep-water routes beside Timor, the Ombai and Wetar Straits. These two strategic reasons keep the United States from cutting off all diplomatic ties with Indonesia.

Australia's position that East Timor belongs to Indonesia remains unchanged. Over the years, Australia has given *de facto* recognition to Indonesia's occupation of East Timor. This means that, although Indonesia is not the officially recognized government of East Timor, Australia accepts Indonesia's existing rule of the territory as a viable solution that has worked for more than 20 years.

THE EFFORTS OF NGOS

The efforts of several international nongovernmental

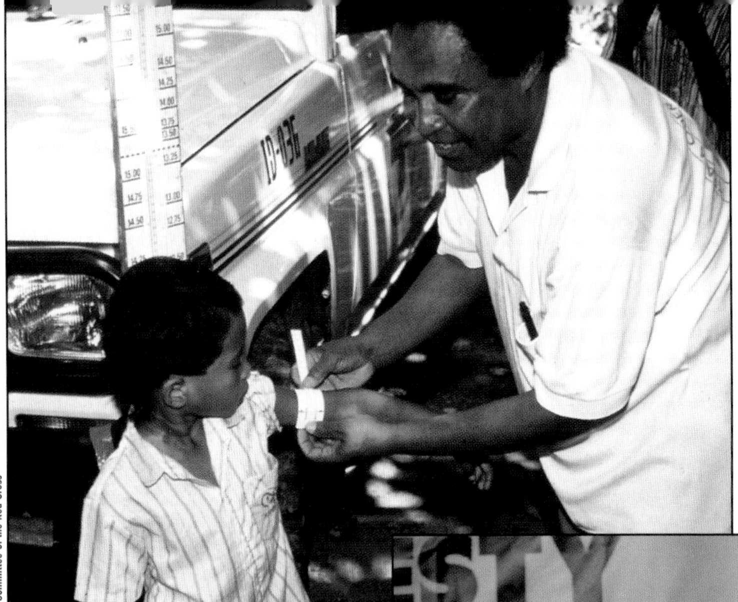

International Committee of the Red Cross

The Red Cross is one of the few organizations allowed to provide humanitarian aid in East Timor. Left: *A Red Cross worker performs a routine checkup on a young East Timorese boy.* Below: *At an Amnesty International conference in Thailand, a speaker shows evidence of violence in East Timor and Indonesia. The group is dedicated to exposing human rights violations across the globe.*

Reuters/Apichart Weerawong/Archive Photos

organizations (NGOs) have been extremely significant in promoting East Timor's cause. NGOs take a stand but don't have a government affiliation. Whereas governments and official third parties such as the UN aren't allowed to intervene in national conflicts without consent from the parties involved, NGOs can step in at the invitation of citizen or rebel groups. Some NGOs provide humanitarian aid, others watch for human-rights violations, and still others petition their own governments and the UN to take political action in solving a conflict.

Humanitarian aid organizations—such as the Red Cross and the Australian Council for Overseas Aid (ACFOA)—supply food, medicine, and clothing to the victims of war or disaster. The International Committee of the Red Cross (ICRC) was formed to protect victims of war. In East Timor, the ICRC interviews political prisoners and monitors the conditions of the sites where they are held.

Groups like Amnesty International and Human Rights Watch/Asia (formerly Asia Watch) focus on human-rights violations. They investigate and publish cases of murder, theft, rape, torture, imprisonment without a fair trial, and other abuses.

Elaine Brière

East Timor has supporters from around the world. In Canada a group of demonstrators protests their government's economic involvement with Indonesia.

Along with these large groups that concern themselves with worldwide human-rights problems, there is a broad international network of human-rights groups in more than 30 countries. The network is interested specifically in East Timor.

A human-rights group will typically interview East Timorese who have left the territory or who have just received a message from friends or relatives still living there. If such people claim to have been abused or to know of abuse, the human-rights group tries to check out the story. This is not easy, because the Indonesian authorities do not allow most human-rights groups—with the occasional exception of the Red Cross—into East Timor. (The Red Cross is not viewed as a threat in most countries because it focuses on humanitarian aid and keeps all of its findings confidential.) Although not every claim of violence proves to be true, many stories are backed by convincing evidence.

Many human-rights organizations concentrate on trying to improve conditions under Indonesian rule instead of urging Indonesia to leave East Timor. Other groups take a more political role, such as Australia's East Timor Talks Campaign, whose goal is to persuade Portugal, Indonesia, and East Timor to open discussions. Some organizations, including a huge number of groups in Australia, Portugal, Canada, and the United States, campaign against the Indonesian occupation.

For the most part, though, worldwide peace groups have had little effect on Indonesian policies. Groups concentrate on pressuring their own governments to get tough with Indonesia by arranging trade embargoes, by refusing to sell arms, and by

In 1992 a show of international solidarity for the East Timorese took place when Portuguese activists organized a project called the Mission for Peace in Timor. Participants came from around the world to sail aboard the *Lusitania Espresso* from Darwin, Australia, to East Timor. The project's aim was to nonviolently draw media attention to the situation in East Timor. Many of the participants told journalist Andrew MacMillan that they felt guilty about their governments' inaction in the face of the Dili Massacre and felt a moral obligation to do something. They were stopped by Indonesian gunboats off the coast of Dili.

taking an official stance against the Indonesian occupation of East Timor. These groups publicize information about East Timor and urge people to get involved by writing to their government representatives. Most organizations publish newsletters and a mission statement, and many have Internet websites that feature frequent updates about events that affect East Timor.

LOCAL EFFORTS FOR PEACE

Not all peace groups are based outside Indonesia. An Indonesian office of the Red Cross exists in Jakarta, and Indonesian relief workers from various agencies were the first to enter East Timor after the 1975 invasion. There is also a Jakarta-based peace group called the Joint Committee for the Defense of the East Timorese. Indonesian-based human-rights groups cannot be very vocal in their criticism of the Indonesian government for fear of punishment, but their

Speaking Out

Grady Semmens

Isabel Galhos can't remember a time when her life wasn't affected by the Indonesian occupation. She was 3 years old when soldiers entered her home to arrest her father and beat to death her two young brothers. When she was 13, the military came to her school and forced her and her female classmates to get injections.

"They told us we needed to be injected to stay healthy. I was frightened; I didn't trust them," she said. With the help of Bishop Belo, the girls discovered they had been injected with Depo-Provera, a birth control drug. It is rumored that forced sterilization is one tactic used by the government to change the ethnic balance of East Timorese society.

Galhos lived in fear, both for her own safety and for the safety of her friends and family. She wanted to help the situation in her homeland, so in 1989 she joined the underground resistance movement. She helped to organize the demonstration at the cemetery, where many of her classmates would die in the Dili Massacre.

To hide her involvement in the anti-Indonesian movement, Galhos joined the Indonesian youth military corps. She trained with the army for three years, learning to fight against her own people. Meanwhile, she supplied money and information to the resistance.

In 1994 the Indonesian government selected her to represent East Timor in a Canadian-sponsored youth program. She seemed to stand for the well-educated, pro-integration youth of East Timor. Once in Canada, Galhos defected with the help of an uncle, who lived there. She has been touring cities in North America to speak about her homeland. She hopes to influence Canadian and American citizens to persuade their governments to work toward a change in East Timor.

Although the governments of ASEAN members promise not to interfere with one another's domestic affairs, their citizens sometimes take action. On the twentieth anniversary of the invasion, a demonstration in Jakarta (above) *included both East Timorese and Indonesian protesters. The banner reads, "Twenty years of development in East Timor equals 200,000 souls of my people." A student group in Manila, Philippines* (right), *protests the occupation of East Timor.*

existence is a reminder that not all Indonesians agree with how the situation in East Timor has been handled.

Although many politically oriented peace groups consist of non-Timorese citizens, there are organizations composed of East Timorese exiles. The CNRM has offices near Sydney, Australia, and in Darwin, Australia. It also has branches in the Netherlands, Portugal, and the United States.

João Carrascalão, a UDT representative, also maintains an office in Australia and campaigns against the Indonesian occupation. While this might be surprising in light of the UDT's role in the Indonesian takeover, this sort of turnabout is not unusual among people who had once been persuaded to give Indonesia a chance in East Timor but have been disappointed in the results.

The ability of Fretilin (later the CNRM) and the UDT to set up offices outside East Timor has been crucial to keeping alive the resistance movement. After Indonesia invaded in 1975, Ramos-Horta and Mari Alkatiri, among others, sometimes appeared before the UN to state Fretilin's case. As the East Timor issue went onto the international back burner, the political arm of the resistance slipped into greater obscurity but its political advocates abroad continued to have influence among NGOs.

THE CHURCH'S ROLE

Next to the Indonesian government, the organization

Peter Williamson

A congregation pours from a church on Good Friday, a Christian holy day. Catholic Church membership has more than doubled since the 1975 invasion. The church defends the rights of the East Timorese, and also provides a way for them to silently protest their mainly Muslim occupiers.

with the greatest influence in East Timor is the Roman Catholic Church—one of very few organizations in a position to help resolve the East Timor problem. The East Timorese Catholic Church provides sanctuary for endangered citizens, and church officials speak out against the violence. In addition, the East Timorese clergy delivers sermons in Tetum to help preserve East Timorese language and culture.

The East Timorese Catholic Church initially did not want to get involved with the political struggle, but after cooperating with Fretilin members in the mountains during the early years of the occupation, the clergy began to see that the two sides could work together.

Between 1976 and 1988, when Indonesia isolated East Timor, the Catholic Church offered a means of communication with the outside world. Many reports of conditions in East Timor were smuggled out through church channels. In addition, parish priests and nuns who fled to the mountains held religious services for the refugees.

They brought medicine and books from the cities and helped cultivate food to sustain the growing number of refugees. Through the 1990s, the East Timor Catholic Church continued to provide medical treatment to urban victims who can't get help from the official health-care system because they have demonstrated anti-Indonesian feelings.

Members of the Catholic Church outside East Timor support the Catholics still living there. The Australian aid organization ACFOA has a large Catholic membership led by Australian bishop Hilton Deakin. Catholic groups in Britain and the Philippines are also strong campaigners for better treatment of the East Timorese.

Since the invasion, church officials in East Timor have taken a clear position against the Indonesian policy. But the administration in Vatican City (a city-state that serves as the headquarters for the Roman Catholic Church) wants to avoid damaging relations with Muslim communities throughout Southeast Asia and therefore is careful not to offend the Indonesian government. While the pope watches the situation in East Timor with concern, he is careful not to directly criticize the Indonesian occupation. This caution motivated the pope to direct Bishop Belo to work directly with the Vatican rather than under Indonesian jurisdiction. In this position the bishop is able to speak more freely and has more protection for his actions on behalf of the East Timorese. Nevertheless, many East Timorese wish that the pope would take a stronger stand against Indonesia.

Bishop Belo—although unquestionably an opponent of the occupation—has to balance his actions between campaigning for East Timorese self-determination and not riling the Indonesian authorities. If he is too outspoken, the Indonesian government might try to replace him with an Indonesian bishop. Or it might weaken Belo's influence by dividing East Timor into two dioceses and placing a second bishop in charge.

The Indonesian government has attempted to use the East Timorese people's respect for the clergy to its advantage. Its hope is that, with an Indonesian priest, the East Timorese Catholic Church would become less involved in the struggle. But through the years, the Catholic Church has come to stand in part for East Timorese identity. Even Indonesian priests who might

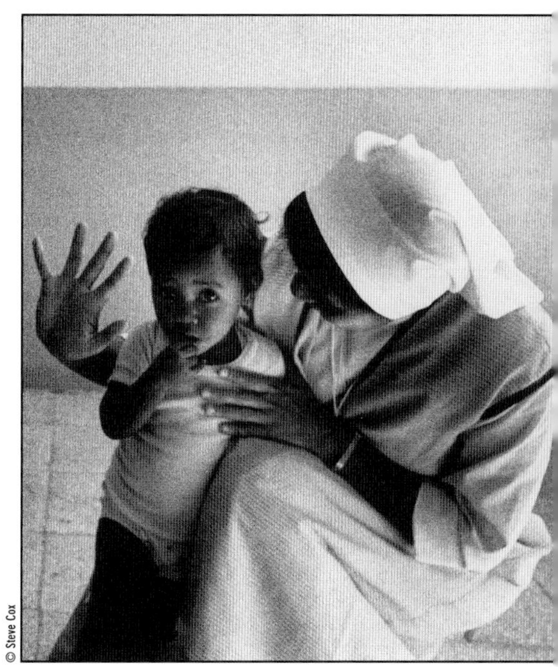

© Steve Cox

A Catholic nun with a young orphan of the occupation waves at a photographer.

personally sympathize with the struggle are seen as symbols of domination by Indonesia. Some East Timorese would rather walk for hours to a neighboring parish just to hear Mass in Tetum from a Timorese priest than to hear it from an Indonesian priest.

> *"By spending more money per capita on development in East Timor than in any other province . . . Indonesia has built more roads, bridges, schools and clinics here than Portugal did during its . . . years of colonial rule."*

UNCERTAINTY PREVAILS

It's unlikely that the problem in East Timor will be solved militarily. Indonesia still hopes that when enough time has gone by, the international community will have forgotten about East Timor, and the East Timorese will be more at ease with their situation.

Meanwhile, the Indonesian government strives to assimilate East Timorese into Indonesian culture. They are educated by Indonesian teachers in Bahasa Indonesia, they must adhere to Indonesian law, and they are exposed to Indonesian business and social practices. And finally, as the material benefits of Indonesian occupation—roads, hospitals, universities, and electrical power—spread further, the people, so the government

© Steve Cox

Parishioners are willing to stand outside a church just to hear sermons given in Tetum. Over the years, Catholicism has come to be associated with Timorese identity.

hopes, will be less likely to oust the providers of these comforts. According to this scenario, East Timorese acceptance of Indonesian rule can't be far off.

Many East Timorese feel differently. They continue to rebel against Indonesian rule and still struggle to hold a referendum. They see that the Suharto regime, although it has ruled for more than 30 years, can't rule forever and hope that the next Indonesian administration may not be as willing to strong-arm the East Timorese. Not every Indonesian sees much value in expending state resources—both human and material—to subjugate the people of a not particularly rich outer province. If, because of the East Timor issue, international pressure limited the business opportunities of Indonesia's middle class, a post-Suharto government might have to pay attention. International pressure—represented by the outcry over the Dili Massacre—has already modified Indonesian behavior to some degree. Troops are still occasionally brutal, but they've curtailed their freewheeling ways somewhat since 1991.

Elaine Briére

East Timor activists hang a banner expressing the sentiment that both governments and individuals have to join forces to make a difference in East Timor.

Whether outside influences could actually force the Indonesian government to allow a free and fair vote in East Timor on self-determination seems doubtful. A convergence of many unlikely circumstances would have to occur, some of which would be very unpleasant—perhaps a ruling against the Timor Gap Treaty, perhaps a political upheaval in Indonesia, perhaps some fresh massacre in East Timor, followed by a cutoff of arms sales by the United States and Britain. The East Timorese would like something less catastrophic to change their lives and restore peace to their island.

EPILOGUE*

Conditions in East Timor had changed little by early 1998. Indonesia's military presence remained strong, and security forces continued to clash with anti-Indonesian protesters and guerrillas.

After violence peaked during the weeks surrounding the sixth anniversary of the Dili Massacre, José Ramos-Horta took an unprecedented stand. He recommended that East Timorese resistance fighters call for a cease-fire. On January 3, 1998, guerrilla leader Konis Santana sent a proposal to Jakarta. By mid-January, he was still awaiting a response.

On the diplomatic front, progress toward a solution remained slow. UN-sponsored intra-Timorese talks and dialogues between Indonesia and Portugal reached an impasse. Local politics took a turn, however, when some former members of the Indonesian-installed government in East Timor established the Movement for Reconciliation and Unity of the People of East Timor in December 1997. The group's formation hurt the goal of integration supporters because its founders, originally in favor of integration, became opposed to Indonesian rule.

Meanwhile, political and financial instability besieged Indonesia. After battling enormous forest fires that threatened the region's safety and that drained financial resources, Indonesia's economy took a dive. Growing fears about job insecurity and economic decline, coupled with rumors of President Suharto's failing health, created an atmosphere of civil unrest. In addition, the opposition questioned Suharto's 30-year rule for the first time, suggesting that he step down before presidential elections in March 1998. It remains to be seen what impact these changes might have on the situation in East Timor.

*Please note: The information presented in *East Timor: Island in Turmoil* was current at the time of the book's publication. For the most up-to-date information on the conflict, check for articles in the following weekly publications: *National Catholic Reporter* (US), *The Economist* (UK), and *New Statesmen* (UK). You may also wish to access, via the Internet, Reg.Easttimor News Summaries, a news group that publishes weekly updates exclusively on East Timor, at http://shel.ihug.co.nz/~calliope/Nettalk.html/.

CHRONOLOGY

ca. A.D. 1400s Islam spreads throughout Indonesian archipelago by Arab traders.

ca. 1500 Portuguese merchants increase trade with the Spice Islands located northwest of Timor.

1512 Portuguese traders land on Timor Island.

1520 Portuguese establish a stopover point for traders at Lifau in the present-day district of Ocussi.

1566 Portuguese set up their first permanent settlement near Timor on the island of Solor.

1702 Portuguese establish their first permanent settlement on Timor Island at Lifau. They battle with the neighboring Topass settlement for control of the area.

1769 Because of repeated raids by the Topasses, the Portuguese move their settlement to Dili.

1792–1815 Napoleonic Wars draw Dutch and Portuguese attention away from Timor. The island falls into disrepair.

1815 Dutch and Portuguese agree on present-day boundaries of Timor Island. (They become official when an agreement is ratified in 1913.) With the introduction of coffee as a cash crop, Portuguese presence on the island begins to grow.

1912 Portuguese colonizers put down a 16-year rebellion by East Timorese islanders.

1939–1945 World War II rages in the Pacific. In 1942 East Timorese and an Australian commando unit, Sparrow Force, defend the island from Japanese attacks. After the Australians are evacuated, Japan occupies the island for the duration of the war.

1949 The Republic of Indonesia gains independence from the Dutch and lays claim to all former Dutch territories. Portugal retains its hold in East Timor.

1974 A coup in Lisbon, Portugal, leads to new legislation that allows unions to form in Portuguese colonies. The UDT, Apodeti, and Fretilin form in East Timor.

1975 The UDT and Fretilin form an anti-integration coalition, which breaks apart later in the year. Fretilin puts down a UDT-Apodeti coup and, after the Portuguese retreat to a nearby island, declares independence. On December 5, President Ford and Secretary of State Henry Kissinger meet privately with President Suharto. Indonesia invades East Timor on December 7. Many civilians and Fretilin members retreat to the East Timor interior and conduct a small-scale guerrilla war against Indonesian troops.

1976 In January Indonesia establishes a provisional government in East Timor with members of the UDT and Apodeti. In April Indonesian soldiers suppress a UDT revolt. A governmental assembly petitions Indonesia's President Suharto for integration, which is granted on July 17. Visiting foreign relief workers report 100,000 people killed since the invasion. Suharto closes East Timor to international visitors.

1977 Fretilin continues to fend off the Indonesian army's offensive, retaining control of the territory's interior, where Fretilin distributes food and medicine to citizens who fled the invasion. The Indonesian military begins its encirclement and annihilation campaign (1977–1979).

1978 The Australian government declares its support of Indonesia. The Indonesian army continues its violence against the East Timorese, effectively crippling Fretilin's guerrilla movement. Key members of Fretilin are captured or killed by Indonesian forces.

1979 The Red Cross begins a relief program in East Timor. Reports reveal widespread starvation within resettlement camps and the destruction of crops and water supplies.

1980 Indonesia begins its transmigration campaign to bring Indonesian settlers to East Timor.

1981 East Timorese men are recruited by Indonesian security forces to participate in the "fence of legs" operation. In September Indonesian soldiers kill 500 people in the town of Lacluta.

1982 Apostolic administrator, Bishop Costa Lopes, reports 500 deaths in Lacluta—the largest massacre in East Timor since the invasion. Pope John Paul II states that Vatican City does not approve of the Indonesian annexation of East Timor.

1983 Bishop Costa Lopes angers Indonesian authorities with his outspokenness and resigns, to be replaced by Bishop Belo. A two-month cease-fire between Fretilin forces and the Indonesian military halts fighting, but combat resumes shortly after an Australian delegation visits the area. The Red Cross stops its aid program as fighting escalates.

1985 Australia and Indonesia initiate talks to explore the Timor Gap. Indonesia and Portugal meet formally for the first time since the invasion. Attacks continue between Indonesian soldiers and Fretilin guerrillas.

1988 Several governmental organizations, including the EC, the European Parliament, and the U.S. Congress, support the UN in condemning Indonesia's occupation of East Timor. In response to a request from the East Timorese governor João Carrascalão, Suharto makes plans to reopen the territory in January 1989. Indonesia grants East Timor equal status as a province with the rest of the Republic of Indonesia.

1989 International visitors are allowed into the territory for the first time since 1976. Reports of disease, food shortages, and tight security around resettlement camps are published. Indonesian soldiers use force to disperse a demonstration after a mass given by Pope John Paul II. Foreign journalists witness the scene. Australia and Indonesia sign the Timor Gap Treaty.

1990 Foreign diplomats and tourists witness Indonesian violence against the East Timorese when Indonesian soldiers violently disperse a group of students trying to talk with U.S. ambassador John Monjo outside his hotel.

1991 Foreign governments and organizations continue to decry the Indonesian occupation. Anti-integration activist, Sebastião Gomes, is killed in an attack by pro-integrationist youth. His death and the cancellation of a visit from a Portuguese delegation lead to the Dili Massacre on November 12.

1992 Indonesian soldiers arrest Fretilin leader and anti-integration icon Xanana Gusmão on November 20. He is sentenced to 20 years in a Jakarta prison.

1994 The conflict takes on visibly more ethnic and religious tones as Indonesian soldiers desecrate sacred Catholic wafers by spitting them out. Later in the year, the murder of an East Timorese by an Indonesian transmigrant spurs ethnic clashes. The number of anti-integration demonstrations by East Timorese rises.

1995 First set of UN-sponsored intra-Timorese talks takes place in June. The International Court of Justice decides it cannot rule on the Timor Gap case.

1996 The second set of UN-sponsored intra-Timorese talks are held in April. Bishop Belo and José Ramos-Horta receive the Nobel Peace Prize for their work in East Timor. East Timorese rebel leader, Konis Santana, offers a cease-fire.

1997 Santana concedes to a loose association between East Timor and Indonesia in the interest of getting talks moving. Parliamentary elections in Indonesia spur more violence in East Timor. Clashes between East Timorese youth and Indonesian security forces continue.

SELECTED BIBLIOGRAPHY

Budiardho, Carmel and Liem Soei Liong, *The War Against East Timor.* London: Zed Books Ltd., 1984.

Carey, Peter and G. Carter Bently, *East Timor at the Crossroads: The Forging of a Nation.* Honolulu: University of Hawaii Press, 1995.

Cox, Steve and Peter Carey, *Generations of Resistance: East Timor.* London: Cassell, 1995.

Indonesia in Pictures. Minneapolis: Lerner Publications Company, 1990.

Injustice, Persecution, Eviction: A Human Rights Update on Indonesia and East Timor, March 1990. N.p.: The Asia Watch Committee, 1990.

Jolliffe, Jill, *East Timor Nationalism and Colonialism.* St. Lucia, Australia: University of Queensland Press, 1978.

Ramos-Horta, Jose, *Funu: The Unfinished Saga of East Timor.* New Jersey: The Red Sea Press, Inc., 1987.

Taylor, John G., *Indonesia's Forgotten War: The Hidden History of East Timor.* New Jersey: Zed Books Ltd., 1991.

INDEX

ABOUT THE AUTHOR

Taro McGuinn, an expert in Asian affairs, is an American who has lived in Southeast Asia for several years.

ABOUT THE CONSULTANTS

Andrew Bell-Fialkoff, *World in Conflict* series consultant, is a specialist on nationalism, ethnicity, and ethnic conflict. He is the author of *Ethnic Cleansing,* published by St. Martin's Press in 1996, and has written numerous articles for *Foreign Affairs* and other journals. He is writing a book on the role of migration in the history of the Eurasian Steppe. Mr. Bell-Fialkoff lives in Bradford, Massachusetts.

Elizabeth Traube conducted field research among the Mambai of East (formerly Portuguese) Timor between 1972 and 1974. She is the author of *Cosmology and Social Life: Ritual Exchange among the Mambai of East Timor* (Chicago: University of Chicago Press, 1986).

SOURCES OF QUOTED MATERIAL

p. 47 José Ramos-Horta, *Funu: The Unfinished Saga of East Timor* (New Jersey: The Red Sea Press, Inc., 1987), 21. Quoting Alfred Russel Wallace, *The Malay Archipelago* (London: MacMillan, 1869); p. 50 José Ramos-Horta, *Funu: The Unfinished Saga of East Timor* (New Jersey: The Red Sea Press, Inc., 1987), 30; p. 62 Bishop Carlos Ximenes Belo, "After Years of Suffering, People in East Timor Want Real Change," *Minneapolis Star Tribune,* 12 Dec. 1996, 27A; p. 63 Robert L. Barry, "An Errant Nobel Peace Prize," *The Washington Post,* 29 Oct. 1996, A17; p. 67 Hupudio Supardi, "Indonesia on East Timor," (letter to the editor) *The Washington Post,* 15 Mar. 1997, A22; p. 69 East Timor *Action* Network, *Background on East Timor and U.S. Policy* (Washington D.C.: East Timor *Action* Network/U.S., April 1997); p. 81 William Branigin, "E. Timorese Chafe Under Foreign Yoke," *The Washington Post,* 27 Apr. 1994, A25.